ROW YOUR BOAT

CUBAN REFUGEE

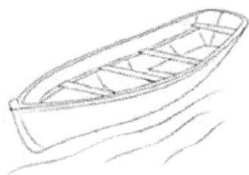

A MEMOIR

CELIA E. OCHOA

Row Your Boat Cuban Refugee

Book Cover Designer: Lorissa Padilla

All photos are property of Celia E. Ochoa unless otherwise stated.

ISBN (Paperback): 979-8-9879344-0-1

ISBN (eBook): 979-8-9879344-1-8

For every scared child who once stood in the detention camps.

I hope life has been gentler with you since and that you have found the courage and chance to claim every opportunity that came your way.

Mom, this is for you.

CONTENT WARNING

This memoir contains events and experiences that may be distressing or triggering, including but not limited to:

- *Death and near-death experiences by various means*
- *Suicide by others in the detention camps*
- *Self-harm by others in the detention camps*
- *Mentions of domestic violence by a parent*
- *Mentions of alcoholism by a parent*

Please know that these are all true events from my life. While I hope you will read and engage with this story, your well-being is far more important. If you feel that any of these topics may be triggering for you, please take care of yourself first and read at your own pace.

AUTHORS NOTE
PART 1

If you are reading this, I want to thank you from the bottom of my heart for giving this story a chance. Memoirs from someone who isn't a celebrity or widely known can feel like a risk, like no one will care to read them. That makes your time and attention all the more meaningful to me, and I am deeply grateful.

The first time I was encouraged to write our story was in 2009 by my college English Literature professor, Ms. Shane, after I submitted a short non-fiction piece for an assignment. By 2010, about a third of the book had already been written when my laptop was stolen, and I lost it all. Since then, the idea of writing a book remained in the back of my mind, with my family reminding me year after year that I needed to tell this story.

In February 2022, while going through old boxes in my garage, I stumbled across the printed, graded copy of that original college story, written almost thirteen years earlier. On it, my professor had written a note encouraging me to submit it to a magazine. Over the years, she would pull me to the side after class countless times, insisting that I write a book about our experiences. If finding that paper wasn't a sign, I don't know what is.

And I took that sign and ran with it.

Throughout this memoir, you will notice that some people are not mentioned by name. This is intentional. It includes, but is not limited to, my own father. I have not seen or spoken to him in eighteen years, and I have no desire to ever have a relationship with him. Yet, it was impossible to tell this story without including him.

As my blurb primarily centers around him, I wanted to take the time to mention that here as it is by no means my intention to confuse you.

While this is my memoir of events in my life that have forever shaped who I am and how I live, it's important to note that he was the reason we had to leave our hometown and ultimately, the reason why we had to leave our country. He figured out how we could escape, and in that way, he is the reason we survived. That, aside from being half the reason I am in this world, is the one good thing he accomplished in his life. I know this may sound harsh, but please understand he was also the prime example of everything I never wanted to be. He was never a good son, brother, husband, or father. But none of that can erase the fact that, despite everything, he gave us the chance to live the "American Dream."

Every year, on the anniversary of our departure, I search the internet in hopes of finding more information, an article, a post, anything, from someone we knew, whether a fellow refugee, someone we met in the camps, or even one of the soldiers we encountered. For that reason, at the end of this book, you will find a collection of photographs from our time in the Guantánamo Bay Detention Camps.

My hope for you as a reader is that this story will offer a sense of hope, even in the darkest times, and provide insight into an experience that very few have lived through.

Once again, thank you, from the bottom of my heart, for reading this story.

CHAPTER 1

CUBAN REFUGEE

Row, Row, Row Your Boat Cuban Refugee, if you paddle harder maybe
you'll be free."

*It is truly my hope that you sang that in your head and if you didn't, well that's
okay, start over.*

I lost count of how many times I heard that joke, over and over again.
Maybe it was a blessing that, at first, I couldn't even understand it.

When I started school in the United States, I didn't speak a single word of
English. Not one. Well...unless you count the one phrase I proudly repeated
like it was the nicest compliment in the world: "suna ma bish." I know, I
know, not exactly the ideal phrase for a seven-year-old to be tossing around
the hallways. I'd picked it up from military personnel in the detention
camps, completely unaware of what it meant. Naturally, I got in trouble for
saying it. More than once.

During those first months of school in Ithaca, New York, being a refugee
made me an easy target.

I didn't speak the language, I'd just come from detention camps, and to top
it off, my family became the first sponsored Cuban refugees in the area.

The local TV station ran a weeklong feature on us, one segment per week, so by the second week every resident who tuned into local programming knew exactly who we were. Our faces. Our story. Everything.

From the time my family went into hiding in Cuba in 1993 until the day we arrived in Ithaca, I'd never had the chance to go to school. I was supposed to start the very week we left our hometown. So, imagine being seven years old, walking into a classroom for the first time in your life, already terrified, and then finding out you were expected to start in kindergarten. Kindergarten. My stubborn little self wasn't having it. Five-year-olds!? Absolutely not.

Thankfully, because of our refugee status, I was given a choice. They allowed me to start second grade, the grade meant for my age. The deal was simple: if I wasn't caught up by the end of the year, I'd have to repeat it.

So, there I was, two years behind, knowing no English whatsoever…unless you count "suna ma bish."

Those early months were the first glimpse of the work ethic I would grow into as an adult. I pushed myself relentlessly to learn the language. So much so that my hair began falling out in literal handfuls. My mother brushed my hair as gently as she could each morning, doing her best to minimize the amount that would fall out. I remember sitting on the shower floor, sobbing, my palms full of hair. Eventually, she had to take me to a doctor.

The diagnosis? Stress. I was working so hard to catch up, to understand, to belong, that the pressure was physically unraveling me. The doctor told me to slow down. But I didn't. Not until I reached my goal. Only then did my hair finally return to normal.

In just four months of ESOL, English for Speakers of Other Languages, I learned the language almost perfectly. Four months.

Once I understood the infamous joke and everything else that was being said about me, the bullying didn't stop, but it helped to be able to come back with a few words of my own. When I look back at it all, I think the bullying became worse once I was able to understand and speak the language. Maybe it wasn't as amusing to them when I couldn't understand their jokes and cruel words, maybe they enjoyed it more knowing that I knew exactly what they were saying.

What helped me through it all was my ESOL teacher, Emily. She was an instrumental part in me realizing that my refugee status wasn't a flaw, it was a strength. She helped me to understand that I should be proud of where I came from, the struggles that my family overcame and what we had survived. She made me believe that what my family and I had gone through was truly an extraordinary experience and that it was a story that mattered, one worth telling. She believed that it was the part of me that would push me toward success, not hold me back.

And she was right.

During the 1994 Cuban Exodus, so many lives were lost. People died searching for the opportunity at a life in the United States. They lost their lives trying to give themselves a better future and hoping to live the American dream.

For reasons I can't fully explain, whether it be luck, fate, or divine intervention, out of more than thirty-five thousand refugees that escaped during the Exodus, we made it, we survived.

We were fortunate enough to have the opportunity to live in this country. A country we had only ever dared to dream about.

Even at seven years old, I knew I would spend my life honoring that chance. I knew I wouldn't waste it.

But before all of that, before the bullying, the English lessons, the TV segments, there is the beginning.

And that's where the story truly starts.

CHAPTER 2

GRAND ENTRANCE

Depending on how you choose to see it, you could call me either incredibly unlucky...or unbelievably lucky.

From the moment I was ready to enter the world, life seemed determined to test me. Yet somehow, every close call, every twist in the wrong direction, always found its way back to something good. It's almost as if my life has been a dance between disaster and deliverance.

A few days before I was born, my mother was admitted to an *hogar materna*, a maternal home where women were monitored when complications arose near their due date. Her blood pressure was dangerously high, and her feet were so swollen that every step was painful. For her safety, she was placed under observation.

At six o'clock in the morning on May 1st, 1988, she woke to a loud pop. Her water had broken. Staff rushed her from the maternal home to the hospital, unaware of just how complicated things were about to become.

During labor, doctors discovered I was breeched, positioned feet first. That meant my head, the largest part of a newborns body, would be the last to come out. Normally, that kind of delivery calls for an emergency C-section to avoid dangerous complications like fractures or the baby becoming stuck. My mother was prepped and wheeled into surgery...but I had other plans. I came too quickly for them to ever have the chance to begin. I was ready to come out.

I hadn't taken my first breath yet, and things were already off to a chaotic start. But then, like so many moments in my life, the chaos shifted. I was born without a single complication. In fact, my birth ended up being easier on my mother than my sister's had been.

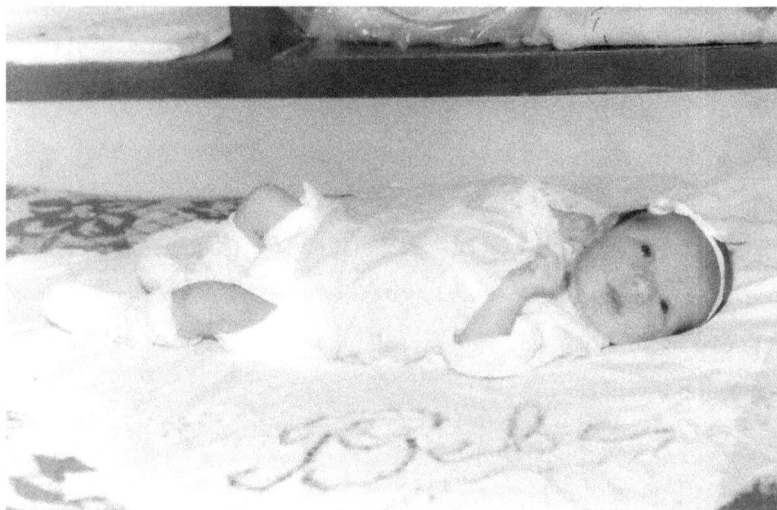

2 MAY 1988 - THE DAY AFTER I WAS BORN
PHOTO PROPERTY OF: CELIA E. OCHOA

My arrival was considered such a significant event that it was announced across our entire province, a place nearly a million people called home in 1988.

Let me explain.

CHAPTER 3

LABOR DAY

In Cuba, my birthday, May 1st, falls on *Día de los Trabajadores*, our version of Labor Day. Every year, the first employed woman to give birth between midnight and 11:59 p.m. in the Province of Holguín won an entire bundle of essentials for her newborn.

And when I say essentials, I mean everything: a crib with its netting, a mattress, an armoire, baskets stuffed with socks, cloth diapers, safety pins, powder, baby cologne, toys…the works.

By the time my mother went into labor, more than six hours had already passed. She assumed the prize had long been claimed, so winning wasn't even something that was on her mind. But the moment she arrived at the hospital, the nurses asked if she was employed. When she said yes, their faces lit up because no one had won yet. Suddenly, it came down to her and one other working woman, both in labor at the exact same time.

Things got complicated when it was discovered that I was positioned feet first and that my mom would need a C-section.

Immediately, the nurses and doctors began arguing: Would a C-section disqualify her? Would it void the prize? Back and forth they went. But I had my own plan. I made my grand entrance first, no C-section needed.

A few hours after I was born, my mother was wheeled out of the delivery room and met by a crowd of people that immediately gave her a dress to put on, they fixed her hair and makeup and gave her a bouquet of roses.

All of this because reporters were on their way to congratulate her and interview her so that they could make the official announcement for the birth of the first worker's baby of the day.

They asked her name, workplace, and municipality. Then they called our town officials to deliver the news: one of their own had won. At that very moment, a Labor Day parade was happening in our town, and over the loudspeakers they announced that Idalmis, an employee of the train terminal, had given birth to a baby girl, born feet first, which in Cuba is considered a sign of good luck.

And just like that, that's how my family learned I'd been born.

And while this all sounds amazing, and it was, nothing in this life is truly 'free'. Everything always comes at a price and there is always a catch. It's that little fine print you typically ignore.

And this one stated something along the lines of, "You win and receive all of the below listed items for free for your newborn but if you would like to claim them you will have to name your daughter Celia or son Ernesto. Should you choose not to name them as such, then you do not receive any of the items."

That was the fine print you couldn't ignore. And that's how I became the only person in my family with a middle name.

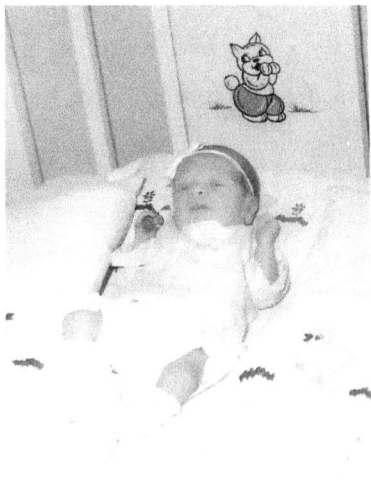

LEFT: 4 MAY 1988 RIGHT: 2 MAY 1988
PHOTOS PROPERTY OF: CELIA E. OCHOA

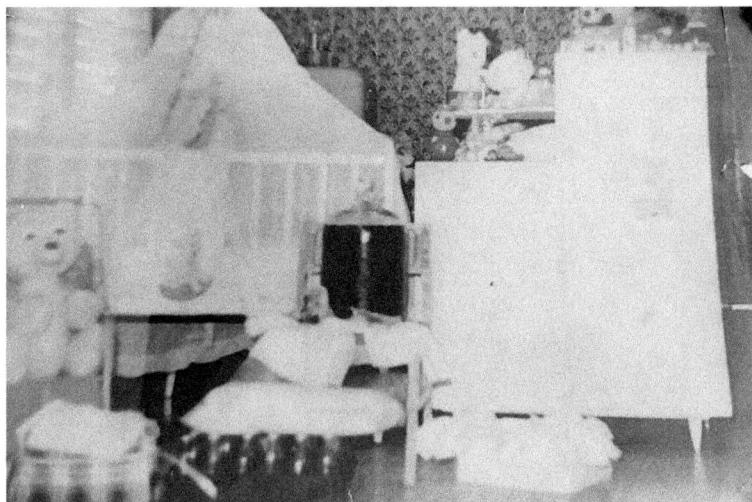

EVERYTHING WE WON
PHOTO PROPERTY OF: CELIA E. OCHOA

In our family, there's a tradition: whatever you name your first-born, every child that follows must have a name that starts with the same letter.

My sister was named Evelyn, so my mom had already picked out the name Elisandra for me long before I arrived. But that one condition, Celia or nothing, ended the tradition, and I unknowingly broke the tradition.

For the first thirteen years of my life, I hated the name Celia. I hated it so much that I went exclusively by my middle name. The irony, of course, is that the name I rejected for so long is the one that came with a story big enough to fill an entire province.

And a lifetime later, I finally understand why.

CHAPTER 4

HAZARDOUS MATERIALS

My streak of being both unbelievably unlucky and impossibly lucky didn't end with my chaotic arrival into the world. If anything, it seemed determined to follow me straight into childhood.

When I was two, at my own birthday party, I darted across the backyard trying to escape my mother's attempts to corral me back inside the house. In my sprint, I tripped, face first, into a piece of sheet metal with its sharp edge curled upward. I still had a pacifier in my mouth and the metal cut straight through it, splitting my lip open.

My mother couldn't get to me quickly enough to stop it from happening, but the second she heard my scream, she was already scooping me off the ground. Her cries joined mine, and within moments the entire party came running outside. I was rushed to the hospital.

The doctor told my parents I was incredibly lucky. The pacifier might have been what saved me as it had acted like a buffer, slowing the impact just enough to keep the metal from going straight through my mouth.

Given my size, the speed I was running, and the sharpness of the metal, it could have been fatal. Another unlucky incident with a lucky ending.

But that wasn't the end of it...

When I was three, I had watched my father on numerous occasions, siphoning gasoline from a truck many times, sucking on a hose until the fuel moved far enough along for him to transfer it into a container.

I didn't understand the mechanics. To my toddler mind, it simply looked like he was drinking from it.

One afternoon, my mother was hanging laundry with her back turned to me. My father had just stepped away from the truck. I wandered out, saw the hose sticking out of the gas tank, and curiosity did the rest. I picked it up, put it to my mouth, and did exactly what I had seen him do.

Except I didn't stop.

When my mother came looking for me, she found me by the truck. She called me over, but as I tried to walk toward her, I wobbled, stumbling with half-closed eyes. By the time I reached the house, I was swaying so hard I could barely stay upright.

She scooped me into her arms immediately, panic erupting. My father ran over, and when she told him where she'd found me, the realization hit him like a blindside blow to the face: I must have picked up the hose and drank from it. Neighbors gathered as my mother cried and screamed for help. A crowd quickly formed.

On the same street that we lived on, there was a warehouse and there was a delivery truck parked in front of it awaiting a shipment. The driver yelled for my parents to get in, he'd take us to the clinic. By then, I was slipping in and out of consciousness. My mother kept shaking me, begging me to stay awake.

Inside the truck, things got worse. My eyes rolled back until only the whites were visible. My mother, frantic, began screaming,

"Está muerta…mira…mi niña se murió."
She's dead…look…my baby is dead.

My father checked for a pulse. He couldn't find one.

I was gone.

Instinct took over him. He pulled me from my mother's arms and began CPR. It was the longest minute of their lives.

And then, just like you would see in a movie, I gasped, eyes opening, life rushing back in.

Even though my pulse had returned, they still took me to the clinic and then to the hospital for further testing. They pumped my stomach, ran every exam they needed to, and kept me under observation until they were certain I was okay.

And in the end, miraculously, I was okay. No lasting damage. No complications. Nothing to indicate that I had in fact died for over a minute.

It was as if something, or someone, was watching over me that day. Another impossibly lucky ending to an otherwise terrifying story.

CHAPTER 5

WAR HERO OCHOA

To understand one of the biggest factors that pushed my family to escape Cuba, I need to take you back to July 13th, 1989.

That date matters because it was the day General Arnaldo Ochoa, once celebrated as a national war hero, was executed by firing squad.

And why does his death matter to my story? Because General Arnaldo Ochoa was my father's cousin.

At dawn, inside the *Tropas Especiales* military base in Baracoa, Guantánamo, he gave the command for his own execution. He refused a blindfold, insisted on facing his final moment with dignity, and Fidel Castro granted those requests.

GENERAL ARNALDO OCHOA
PHOTO IS A SCREEN CAPTURE FROM THE
TELEVISED TRIAL

25

The official history books will tell you that General Arnaldo Ochoa was guilty of drug trafficking, corruption, and mismanagement of economic resources. While I'm not here to rewrite the history that millions have been taught, I can tell you with absolute certainty that nothing could be further from the truth.

The reality was far more sinister.

Rumors were swirling internationally that the Castro brothers were facilitating drug routes for Colombian cartels, having Cuba serve as a transit point enroute to the United States. In the end, they needed a scapegoat, someone powerful enough to make a statement, but isolated enough to sacrifice.

Arnaldo, being Cuba's most decorated and trusted general, had become too beloved. Crowds applauded when he walked by. His popularity grew to a level that made Fidel and Raúl deeply uncomfortable. A man admired by the masses becomes, in a dictator's eyes, a threat.

He became the perfect fall guy.

They blamed him for everything and claimed to know nothing themselves.

GEN. ARNALDO OCHOA AND FIDEL CASTRO
COPYRIGHT: TRANSLATING CUBA, 18 JULY 2017
https://translatingcuba.com/the-day-they-shot-ochoa/

From that moment on, having any association with him or carrying the Ochoa name in Cuba was like walking around with a target on your back. That is the reality my family suddenly found themselves living in.

I was only fourteen months old when the execution took place and being that young, I have no memory of him at all. All I have are the stories that have been passed down. But the consequences of his death have followed our family across generations.

What I can tell you is that the significance of this is so extreme that to this day, my older sister Evelyn still gets questioned every time she visits Cuba. Immigration officers always ask the exact same thing: "Do you have any relation to Arnaldo Ochoa?"

During one trip in 2009, they detained her for three hours the moment she landed, interrogating her simply because she shared the same last name as a man who was killed when she was just seven years old.

Three hours of questioning. Fifteen years after she left the country. All because of a name.

I share this to show you the magnitude of what staying in Cuba would have meant for us. Remaining there wasn't just dangerous, it was impossible. Our family's fate had already been written the moment the Castro brothers pulled the trigger on Arnaldo Ochoa.

And that is why we had to leave.

CHAPTER 6

LIFE IN CACOCUM

Our life in Cacocum can be summed up in a single word: *tragic.*

PHOTO PROPERTY OF: CELIA E. OCHOA

I wouldn't be able to pinpoint the exact moment I first witnessed my father's violence. When I reach back into the fog of my earliest years, I find blurred fragments, images of myself, no older than two, standing in a doorway while my father beat my mother. I can remember crying, begging him to stop.

And yet, even now, I'm not entirely sure if that memory is real or if it's something my mind pieced together from the countless incidents that followed. My mother, too, struggles to recall each one. There were simply too many.

Most of his brutality came on drunken nights but even sober he found ways to break us. His words were weapons. His presence alone could change the energy of a room. And my mother, my poor mother, always received the worst of it.

When she was pregnant with me, she remembers him kicking her in the back. Other times he dragged her by the hair, slapped her across the face, or threatened her life if she dared to leave.

As my sister and I grew older, we weren't spared. We too experienced his abuse. My sister, six years older than me, caught the brunt of it. She started rebelling young, something I didn't understand at the time but fully recognize now as survival. Her defiance only fueled his rage, and she paid for it more than any of us.

His punishments were cruel and calculated. The most common punishment was forcing us to kneel on raw grains of rice for hours.

If he walked by and our backs weren't perfectly straight, he'd whip us, sometimes with a belt, sometimes with his hands.

Either way, the result was always the same: welts and bruises that stayed with us for weeks.

As his violence escalated, my mother tried to leave him more than once. She sought refuge with her parents, hoping each time that it would finally be over. But one afternoon he showed up at my grandparents' home and told my grandmother that if my mother didn't return to him, he would bring her daughter's head to her on a plate.

So my mother went back. Fear left her no other choice.

This was our reality.

The weight of the name Ochoa in our town, already a name under scrutiny, made even heavier by my father's chaos. There was no laying low, no flying under the radar. The spotlight found us whether we wanted it or not.

And with everything mounting around us, what happened next, what we were ultimately driven to do, felt inevitable.

OUR HOME IN CACOCUM
PHOTO PROPERTY OF: CELIA E. OCHOA

INTERIOR OF OUR HOME
PHOTO PROPERTY OF: CELIA E. OCHOA

CHAPTER 7

CACOCUM - 1993

In Cacocum, a small municipality in the province of Holguín, electricity was not a convenience, it was a constant source of frustration. Power outages were relentless, arriving without warning and lingering for hours. The worst of them came at night. The lights would vanish, and with them any hope of relief, often not returning until morning. Dinner was frequently eaten in near-total darkness, candles flickering at every corner of the table. Sleep offered no escape. We lay in pools of sweat, skin peppered with mosquito bites, listening to the heavy stillness of a town without power.

One evening, as we sat down to eat, the electricity failed yet again. My father, impatient, impulsive, and already simmering, erupted. His anger was instant and consuming. I watched his pupils expand until the brown of his eyes seemed to disappear entirely, swallowed by rage. It was a look we knew too well, one we had learned to fear.

Without thinking, without restraint, he began to shout.
"Vete pa la mierda, Fidel, hijo de puta."
Fuck you, Fidel, you son of a bitch.

The blackout had plunged the entire town into silence, and in that silence, his words carried. There was nothing to mask them, no radios, no televisions, no hum of electricity. Every neighbor could hear him clearly. One of them, unfortunately, was a member of the PCC - *the Partido Comunista de Cuba*. As expected, a report was made. The next day, my father was arrested. He spent three days in jail before being released. It wasn't his first arrest, and it would not be his last. He had a long and troubled history with the police.

Like most young men in Cuba, my father had served in the military. His service can be summed up simply: authority and he did not coexist peacefully. Add to that his last name, Ochoa, linking him to General Arnaldo Ochoa, and he became an easy target. His record only worsened with time: drunken outbursts, verbal tirades, domestic violence, disorderly conduct. Each incident added another mark to an already dangerous file.

When a lawyer was finally hired and my father appeared in court, the truth became impossible to ignore. The government intended to sentence him to ten to twenty years in prison. An appeal was immediately filed in Holguín and then pushed all the way to the Supreme Court of Cuba. But the lawyer chose honesty over false hope. He told us plainly that the appeal would lead nowhere. It was not meant to win; it was meant to delay. Time, he explained, was the only thing he could give us.

Time to disappear. Time to plan. Time to escape. He told us that if there was any way, any way at all, to leave Cuba, we had to do it immediately.

And just like that, the life we knew began to unravel. From that moment on, nothing was wasted, not a day, not a decision, not a second. Everything moved toward one inevitable truth:

We were running out of time.

CHAPTER 8

HAVANA - 1993

My father began planning immediately. There was no room for hesitation, and certainly none for mistakes. Every move had to be calculated, quiet, and invisible.

His cousin Teresa and her husband, Serjito, were living in Cacocum at the time, but they owned a small, unoccupied one-bedroom apartment in Havana. Serjito agreed to let us stay there for a few months, just long enough, we hoped, to find a way out of the country.

The apartment was located in East Havana, in an area known as *La Rotonda de Cojímar.* The Roundabout of Cojímar.

LA ROTONDA DE COJIMAR
COPYRIGHT: GOOGLE MAPS

My father began planning immediately. There was no room for hesitation, and certainly none for mistakes. Every move had to be calculated, quiet, and invisible.

His cousin Teresa and her husband, Serjito, were living in Cacocum at the time, but they owned a small, unoccupied one-bedroom apartment in Havana. Serjito agreed to let us stay there for a few months, just long enough, we hoped, to find a way out of the country.

The apartment was located in East Havana, in an area known as La Rotonda de Cojímar – the Roundabout of Cojímar.

In June 1993, under the cover of darkness, we prepared to leave our home in Cacocum. We owned a 1956 Buick, and we crammed into it everything we could carry: clothes, photographs, important documents, small pieces of our past, and our dog. Given the danger of our situation, every precaution mattered. We could not be seen. Especially not by our neighbor.

Havana was the destination not only because we had a place to hide, but because it was the closest point to the United States. Once there, we would figure out the rest.

That first night, we didn't make it far.

The Buick began to fail under the weight of our lives packed into its trunk and backseat. It had never been pushed that hard before, and neither had we.

With no other choice, we turned around and crept back home, hearts pounding the entire way.

My father was a skilled mechanic, and within two days he had the car running again. Once more, in the dead of night, we loaded everything back in and set out. This time, we didn't stop. After nearly fifteen exhausting hours on the road, we arrived at Serjito's apartment in Havana.

In Cuba, your home was registered with your municipality. That registration determined your monthly food rations, rice, sugar, oil, soap, and a few basic necessities, allocated per person. But we were fugitives of circumstance, hiding in a borrowed apartment. We were not registered. Which meant we had no rations at all.

We arrived in Havana with very little money. Some days, we didn't eat. When hunger became unbearable, we walked to a nearby diner and bought the cheapest thing on the menu. It was a yellowish, wet, sticky rice dish that I didn't know at the time was mixed with shark meat. It smelled like days-old urine and tasted no better. But it was all we could afford, and so we ate it, often.

Slowly, as days passed, we learned the rhythm of the neighborhood. The fear softened just enough to breathe. The unfamiliar began to feel almost normal. In time, the apartment started to feel like a temporary version of home.

Even our dog adjusted.

One afternoon, we took him with us to a nearby neighborhood called *Villa Panamericana*. On the walk back, he suddenly bolted. We searched for hours, frantic and desperate. I cried the entire time. When we finally gave up and returned to the apartment, there he was, sitting calmly at the front door, as if nothing had happened. Pupper had found his way home.

A few weeks later, he ran off again.

This time, he never came back.

And just like that, another piece of our old life was gone.

CHAPTER 9

SACRIFICES

While we were hiding in Havana, family members in Cacocum continued to collect our food rations on our behalf. For a time, that fragile system kept us going.

But money, like everything else, eventually ran out. There came a point when there was simply no way to buy food. Hunger stopped being an inconvenience and became an emergency. My parents were forced into another impossible decision. In the dead of night, they would have to drive back to Cacocum to retrieve the rations themselves. It was an extraordinarily dangerous risk.

By then, the authorities in our hometown knew we were gone. They knew we were running. But the choice was brutal and simple: starve or take the risk. So, they went.

Against the odds, they made the trip safely and returned with what we needed to survive. For a brief moment, we could breathe again. But even those rations were finite. When they ran out, we were once again at the edge. Another sacrifice became unavoidable.

The 1956 Buick, the car that had carried us out of Cacocum under cover of darkness, had to be sold. For my father, a skilled mechanic in a country where owning a car was a rarity, this was not just transportation. It was pride. It was identity. It was security.

Letting it go nearly broke him.

The Buick sold for 23,000 Cuban pesos, which, after conversion, amounted to an almost unbelievable $191.67.

That was the price of survival.

COPYRIGHT: BARRETT-JACKSON
https://www.barrett-jackson.com/Events/Event/Details/1956-BUICK-SPECIAL-2-DOOR-COUPE-130322

CHAPTER 10

BETRAYED

As the search for a way out of Cuba continued, my father met with a man rumored to have 'connections'. Someone who claimed he could coordinate an escape. But the moment the meeting ended, my father knew something was wrong. He couldn't explain it, only that the man's words didn't sit right. Trust, in those days, was a gamble that often ended in prison, and his instincts told him this man could not be trusted.

Around the same time, my aunt Magalis, my uncle Roget, and my cousin Yulicer were living in Havana, also desperate to leave the country. For a brief moment, hope took shape. A plan came together for all of us to escape at once. The money was gathered. The date was set. Every detail was arranged. Then, at the last possible moment, it collapsed.

Like so many others driven by desperation, we were scammed and betrayed. Someone had informed the authorities. The escape we believed in was never real. Had we arrived at the meeting point, we would have walked straight into an ambush. Arrest would have been inevitable. By sheer luck, we learned the truth before it was too late.

With the failed plan went every peso we invested. This kind of betrayal had become common across the country. The same people paid to organize escapes often pocketed the money and alerted the authorities instead. We lost everything, but not our freedom. Eventually, with no money left and no new path forward, my aunt, uncle, and cousin made the painful decision to return to Cacocum.

Time continued to slip by. Months passed with no progress, no plan, and no certainty.

By December of 1993, we had far exceeded the two to three months we were supposed to stay in Serjito's apartment. The unspoken tension became unavoidable. He needed his home back, and we had nowhere else to go. Another move became necessary. My father's cousin Fidelito's in-laws owned a modest house on the beach in Mayabeque. The area was known for its murky waters, said to carry medicinal and healing properties. Whether that was true or not hardly mattered. What mattered was that it offered shelter.

And so, once again, we packed what little we had left and moved, still searching, still waiting, still hoping, for a way out.

CHAPTER 11

MAYABEQUE

Living in Mayabeque felt like a dream come true. At least, it would have been if we hadn't been on the run. Fear still followed us, a quiet companion that never fully loosened its grip. We were always listening, always watching, always aware that safety could be taken from us in an instant. But despite that, Mayabeque offered something we hadn't felt in a long time: *relief.*

The house sat on a beautiful stretch of beach, far enough from town to give us a sense of privacy, even protection. For the first time in months, we weren't constantly looking over our shoulders. The ocean provided what money could not. Food was plentiful, fresh, and dependable. The sea fed us when everything else had failed.

Some of my happiest memories were made there, wading into the water to set fishing nets, returning hours later to pull them in heavy with fish. Those nets became dinner not just for one night, but for days.

For the first time since we went into hiding, we didn't have to worry about whether we would eat.

PLAYA MAYABEQUE
PHOTO PROPERTY OF: GOOGLE MAPS

We swam in the ocean whenever we wanted, letting the water wash away at least some of the weight we carried. The simple luxury of floating, laughing, breathing without fear of hunger felt unreal.

Having food, shelter, and a moment of peace eased the pressure that had been crushing our family. In Mayabeque, we finally found stability, even if it was temporary. And with that stability came clarity. For the first time, survival was no longer the only goal. Now, we could focus on what mattered most: *Finding a way out.*

CHAPTER 12

STRANGER AT OUR DOOR

Because it was winter, most of the houses along Mayabeque beach sat empty. From time to time, my mother, my sister Evelyn, and I stayed there alone while my father traveled to Havana. He went for whatever odd jobs he could find to save money, but also to continue searching for a way out.

The three of us slept together on a single mattress laid out on the floor in the middle of the sparsely furnished living room. It was how we felt safest, close, connected, alert. One of those nights alone became unforgettable.

It was a quiet night, the beach silent. With houses spaced far apart and no outdoor lighting, the darkness was almost complete. The only light filtering into the house came from the moon. For reasons I still can't explain, we didn't fall asleep as quickly as we usually did.

Then it began.

The wooden porch creaked. The sound moved slowly, from one end of the porch to the other. I immediately curled into my mother, my heart pounding so hard I was certain it could be heard. As we lay frozen on that mattress, the footsteps continued, the wood groaning under deliberate weight. My mother wrapped her arms around us and whispered for us to stay absolutely still. Time stretched painfully. The footsteps traveled the length of the porch, lingering. In my mind, I pictured someone stopping at every window, testing every door, searching for an opening. Listening. Watching.

Thankfully, none of the doors or windows were open. Eventually, the creaking stopped. The footsteps faded.

Whoever it was moved away from the house. That night, none of us slept. We stayed awake until morning, listening for any sound that might mean that person had returned. We didn't know if this had happened before, if we had simply slept through it, or if this was the first time we'd been awake enough to notice.

The next day, we learned the truth. There was a peeping tom who frequented the area. He had discovered that a woman and two young girls were living in that house, and that we were often alone. He had been watching us through the windows at night on more than one occasion.

The same wraparound wooden porch, so old and loud that you walked on it half-expecting it to collapse, had betrayed him. Its creaks were the only warning we were ever given. I will never forget that night. The moment that we realized someone had been watching us.

Most of the homes were empty that season. Had that man decided to do more than watch, had he managed to get inside, there would have been no one to hear us. Not a single soul for miles along that beach.

CHAPTER 13

LECHUGA - 1994

The months dragged on with no escape in sight. Hope began to thin, stretched to its breaking point. It started to feel as though we would never find a way out, only remain suspended, waiting to be caught. Trapped in a life that could end at any moment.

We stayed in the house on Mayabeque beach from December of 1993 until March of 1994.

Not far from Mayabeque was a town called Lechuga. A family we knew from Cacocum was living there, and they were eager to return home. They approached us with a proposal: if we were willing to exchange homes, they would take our house in Cacocum, and we could have theirs in Lechuga. We agreed. We needed a place that was ours, something more permanent. House-swapping was common in Cuba. Very few people had the resources to buy a new home whenever life demanded a move. Exchanging houses was often the only practical option.

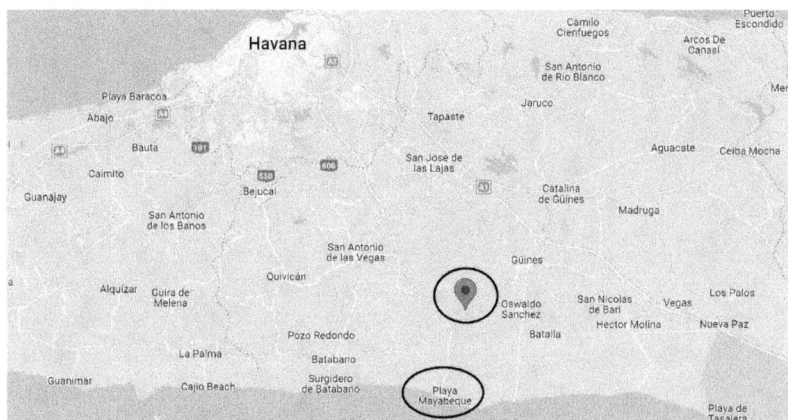

PLAYA MAYABEQUE AND LECHUGA
PHOTO PROPERTY OF: GOOGLE MAPS

63

The best thing about the home in Lechuga was the land itself. The area was known for its fruit trees, and ours did not disappoint. A banana tree stood nearby. Two avocado trees shaded the yard. A massive mango tree loomed over the house, its branches heavy with fruit. After a year of running, of rationing every peso and every bite, these trees felt like a quiet miracle. Just as the ocean had fed us in Mayabeque, the land now sustained us. My mother always had avocados to stretch into meals. We ate mangoes and bananas constantly. If I ever went missing, chances were that you'd find me perched on the roof, eating a mango straight from the skin. I was often there.

But even with food no longer an immediate worry, reality set in. Now that we had something resembling a permanent home, my father knew what had to come next. He needed steady work, some kind of reliable income, to keep us afloat while he continued the relentless search for a way out of the country. Survival was no longer enough. We still needed an escape.

CHAPTER 14

THE FARM

He was able to find a job at a farm where the owner cultivated rice, beans, plantains, and garlic and he also had cows for milk. This was a huge help as he shared these items with us. He also owned several tractors and as my father was a skilled mechanic, he was able to help the owner, Vicente, by fixing his tractors when he had mechanical issues with them.

Over time, respect became friendship. Months passed before my father dared to tell Vicente the truth, that we were on the run, why we were living in Lechuga, and what we were desperately trying to do. Vicente listened carefully. Then he gave one warning: tell no one. Never bring anyone else to the farm. Secrecy was everything. And then he offered something extraordinary. Vicente had a small, unused house on his property. My father could use it to build a boat.

From that moment on, every peso my father earned went toward materials. Piece by piece, he bought metal sheets and steel bars. With his soldering equipment, he began to build the boat from nothing. True to his promise, he worked alone. No help. No witnesses. He became relentless. Any time he was not at the farm, he was inside that small house, soldering, shaping, sealing. The air was thick with heat and metal. Sleep became secondary. The boat consumed him.

The secrecy that kept us safe also came at a cost. The boat could never touch the water before it mattered most. There would be no trial run. No corrections. No second chances. My father would have to trust his hands, his knowledge, and his instincts, and believe that what he was building in silence would carry us to freedom.

PLASTIC MODEL OF OUR BOAT
PHOTO PROPERTY OF: CELIA E. OCHOA

CHAPTER 15

FREE TO LEAVE

On August 5th, 1994, rumors of an illegal boat departure out of Havana prompted Cuban authorities to form a blockade along the Malecón walls. What began as a police operation quickly ignited something far larger.

Thousands of Cubans flooded the streets. The uprising became known as the *Maleconazo*, a spontaneous eruption of decades of desperation. People shouted what had long been forbidden to say out loud. "Libertad." Freedom. "Abajo con los Castros." Down with the Castros. For the first time in generations, fear loosened its grip just enough for truth to spill into the open. The response was brutal and predictable. Protesters were beaten, shot, and arrested in broad daylight. The streets became scenes of chaos and violence. It was the worst civil unrest Cuba had seen in decades.

5 AUGUST 1994 - EL MALECONAZO
COPYRIGHT: DEMOCRATIC SPACES - REMEMBERING EL MALECONAZO
3 AUGUST 2020
https://democraticspaces.com/blog/2020/8/3/remembering-el-maleconazo

And then, in an unexpected and calculated move, Fidel Castro announced a reversal of policy. Anyone who wanted to leave Cuba would be allowed to do so. They would not be stopped. They would not be arrested. There was, of course, a catch.

Any vessel with an engine would be intercepted. Only boats without motors, rafts, makeshift vessels, anything powered by desperation and the sea, would be allowed through. Castro understood exactly what that meant. Reaching the United States without an engine was infinitely more dangerous. And most would not survive the journey. This decision had nothing to do with compassion or freedom. It was strategy.

By opening the floodgates, Castro weaponized his own people, deliberately triggering an immigration crisis meant to overwhelm and antagonize the United States.

And that is exactly what happened. An immigration crisis was born, one fueled by hunger, hope, and the impossible choice between staying trapped or risking everything on open water.

CHAPTER 16

PREPARATIONS

After the government announcement, my father knew time was no longer on our side. The policy allowing Cubans to leave could be reversed at any moment, and if he waited too long, we might never get out. Every hour counted.

Although the law said a boat with an engine would be intercepted, my father made a calculated decision: the boat needed a sidecar motorcycle engine. It was the only way to make the journey faster and safer. We had been hiding, running, and planning this escape for over a year, following the rules now made no sense.

It was his cousin, Fidelito, who ultimately found the engine and arranged for it to be brought to the farm.

Since the announcement had been made, many people now were able to openly talk about wanting to leave and as they were openly able to talk about this, they made it known that they were willing to pay anyone that had a way to get them out.

The announcement had sparked a rush of people eager to leave. With the rules loosened, anyone with a way out could openly negotiate their passage. Some offered staggering sums: a man named Chuchi promised $10,000, another, Luiz, offered money and his motorcycle, and a family of three, Isma, Reynaldo, and their four-year-old daughter, Yamiles, offered their apartment and everything inside it.

Fidelito was left to handle the negotiations. We assumed this meant we would leave with a substantial amount of money, enough to give us a decent start in a new country. We were wrong.

In the end, Fidelito couldn't be trusted and he kept everything, money, motorcycle, apartment, everything. We left with nothing but what we had personally packed onto the boat, and with six additional passengers. The risk had just doubled, making the journey far more dangerous, but we had no choice; we had already committed.

On August 21st, around 10 p.m., we left our home in Lechuga. My father had rented a truck and went with Fidelito to the farm to load the boat, planning to meet us at the drop-off point in *Santa Cruz del Norte*.

MAP OF ESCAPE POINT - SANTA CRUZ DEL NORTE
COPYRIGHT: GOOGLE MAPS

Everyone who had *'paid'* for passage was there, still fearful of authorities despite the new policy, moving cautiously and quietly.

An elderly woman offered her home on the beach as a hiding spot. My mother, my sister Evelyn, and I waited inside while the men lowered the boat from the truck and placed it in the water.

When the signal came, we exited her home, stepped onto the beach, grabbed our bags and life vests, and climbed into the boat.

Keeping in mind that there had been no time to test it. It was a huge gamble as we had no idea if it would even float, let alone carry ten people safely.

In preparation for this journey, during the last year, my father had studied celestial navigation, learning to chart a course to the United States using only the stars and a small compass. In the days leading up to this moment, he had worked tirelessly soldering the boat, installing the motorcycle engine, building oars, securing a gas tank, and reviewing the night sky. Sleep had become a luxury he could not afford.

Everything had led to this night. Everything depended on it.

We were about to set out into the unknown.

CHAPTER 17

22 AUGUST 1994

By the time we were ready to leave, it was nearing 2 a.m. The water was dark and still, the night heavy with anticipation. Almost immediately after we pushed off, my father spotted a Cuban military ship in the distance. His voice was sharp but low: everyone needed to get down and stay absolutely silent until the ship passed. Though leaving was technically allowed, the engine in our boat was grounds for being stopped. One wrong move, and we could be arrested. The minutes stretched, tense and suffocating, until the ship finally disappeared into the horizon. Only then did we allow ourselves to sit back, hearts still racing but slightly relieved.

My father had been running on almost no sleep for days. One of the men aboard suggested he rest, offering to steer the boat in his place. Hesitant but knowing he needed it, my father gave in to exhaustion and fell asleep quickly. Sleep, however, didn't last very long.

As the boat had never been tested in the water, it was not long before we found a small gap in the soldering, water began to seep in, quickly filling the bottom of the boat.

Two of the men aboard immediately started taking turns using a small canister to remove the water. There was no other solution, someone had to be there continuously, dumping water just to keep the boat afloat. Only when that crisis was under control could my father allow himself to rest again.

Once again, his sleep did not last long. He woke up an hour or so later to find that the man left in charge of steering had drifted east along the Cuban coast near Matanzas, far from the northeast course toward Florida.

MAP OF ESCAPE POINT IN RELATION TO EAST COASTLINE TO MATANZAS
COPYRIGHT: GOOGLE MAPS

To make matters worse, the compass had been dropped into the ocean shortly after my father fell asleep. Exhausted and furious, he took control again, relying on the stars and his instincts to navigate us in the right direction.

As we moved further into the night, the water revealed a sobering truth. Makeshift vessels floated around us, rafts made from car tires, inner tubes, and large pieces of wood. The desperation of those trying to escape Cuba was impossible to ignore. Each vessel was a testament to courage, fear, and sheer hopelessness.

From the very start of the journey, both my mother and I became violently ill. We were sick for hours, unable to even hold down water. My father and mother had to check my pulse repeatedly, terrified at how weak I had become. Every moment was a struggle, and yet there was no turning back.

The night stretched on, the waves unrelenting, the boat fragile, and every second felt like a gamble with life itself.

CHAPTER 18

NIGHTMARE

Even after leaving Cuba in the middle of the night just hours earlier, sleep did not come easily. Every time I closed my eyes, I imagined the unknown waiting for me when I woke. But exhaustion eventually overpowered fear, and I drifted into an uneasy slumber. Nothing could have prepared me for what I would see next.

Around 6 a.m., frantic voices jolted me awake. The boat rocked violently beneath me. I opened my eyes and scrambled to my feet, trying to locate the voices and source of the commotion. What I saw made my stomach drop as if I had fallen into a nightmare I could not wake from.

I couldn't decide if this was real or not. Shivers traveled down my spine. Goosebumps rose all over my body. A small raft floated nearby. Two men clung to its sides, half-submerged in the water, their faces etched with sheer terror. I had never seen such desperation in anyone's eyes. Their hands gripped the raft as though it were the only thing keeping them alive.

At first, I could not understand why they struggled so violently. How hard could it be to climb back on? I was only six years old, and the gravity of the situation had not fully sunk in. But it was becoming clear that there was more to this horror movie scene. Then I saw it, the reality of the situation finally hit me.

Something lurked beneath the water, unseen but unmistakable.

Suddenly, I understood the fear in their eyes, the struggle to get back on the raft, and their fear of the water. Their fear was not of the waves, it was of what they glimpsed in the depths. The terror that had overtaken them now washed over me as well.

I stood expressionless, emotionless, and with a deep feeling of helplessness. The fear they felt, I now felt it too. Their desperation was now my own. It was as if I were experiencing it too. My chest tightened, my legs froze, and tears blurred my vision. Their yells echoed in my ears. I blinked, and for a moment, they disappeared. Then I blinked again, and the nightmare resumed, each splash higher than the last, each cry louder, more desperate. Suddenly, my own cries were all that I could hear. I could not bear it. I closed my eyes, wishing the horror would vanish, praying that when I opened them, they would be safe on the raft.

When I finally looked again, they were gone. Just gone. The nightmare ended as abruptly as it had begun. Only a lonely raft floated in the water, the wind howling the only sound left to hear. The once dark blue water was now a dark shade of red.

As this was all unfolding, my father did everything he possibly could to rescue them, even as the other men on the boat continuously yelled at him for trying to help them. We were ahead of them in the water and because of the waves we could not turn around, it was impossible. Not only would we risk the possibility of the waves capsizing us, but if we could have reached them, would our boat have even been able to withstand two additional bodies?

Would we too run the risk of encountering the same unknown creature they were encountering beneath the water? The unknown stretched endlessly before us.

He tried to throw ropes, to reach them, to pull them to safety, but the waves prevented him from getting close. Every attempt failed.

They were just kids, no more than eighteen.

After the shock passed, my sister and I fell back asleep, numb from what we had witnessed. Later, around 9:30 a.m., Evelyn awoke to the playful splashing of dolphins leaping on both sides of our boat. We had heard the stories, dolphins often appear near sharks, but they also protect you. Their presence was terrifying and comforting at the same time. They were our silent guardians.

Around 10 a.m., my mother was resting her head against her knees, still weak from nausea. My father tapped her shoulder softly.

"Idalmis, mira, mira a tu isla una última vez."
"Idalmis, look, look at your island one last time."

She lifted her head to see her home one final time. The tears came instantly, a mix of sorrow, loss, and the weight of leaving everything she had ever known behind.

CHAPTER 19

HOPELESS AT SEA

As the sun climbed higher in the sky, the heat became unbearable. It pressed down on us like a physical weight, baking our skin and our hair. The sharp smell of burnt hair made me gag. Around us, personal items floated on the water, suitcases, clothes, toiletries, and pieces of makeshift rafts, some tied together with no one in sight. Every time we spotted one, we called out, hearts racing, hoping for a response. But there was nothing. Silence. Empty vessels drifting endlessly. All morning long, it repeated, a haunting reminder of how many had not made it.

The heat worsened my condition. I was weak, burning up, and violently ill.

The hole in the soldering continued to let water seep in. The constant bailing, the floating debris, the relentless sun, and the emptiness around us drove the men on our boat toward panic. They paced, shouted, and fumed, rocking the boat with every step. We feared a flip with every reckless movement. Through it all, my father remained calm. His focus never wavered. Tunnel vision had replaced fear; he did not panic.

My mother, on the other hand, was beside herself with worry. She never let go of me, cradling me in her arms, trying to keep me hydrated, but anything I drank came right back up. Her fear was a mirror of my weakness.

The waves began to rise, swelling nine to ten inches above the sides of the boat under the combined weight of the passengers and supplies. The men onboard were useless, panicked, and frantic, leaving the real work to my thirteen-year-old sister.

With determination beyond her years, she took control of the steering handle near the engine, helping guide us through the swelling sea while my father focused on keeping the engine running.

Around 5 p.m., a distant shape appeared on the horizon. One that looked like a car. At first, I thought it was a mirage caused by heatstroke or delirium. But as we drew closer, reality hit: it was a boat, a real, solid boat, unlike anything we had seen. It was a rescue vessel from Hermanos al Rescate, Brothers to the Rescue, an organization dedicated to aiding Cubans fleeing on rafts. The boat was stocked with everything we could have imagined: food, water, medicine, and even a candy-like treatment for dehydration. I desperately needed it, having spent the entire day weakened and sick.

Most of the men on this boat were hallucinating after seven days at sea. They pleaded with us to leave them behind, convinced that rescue would come for them. But my father would not abandon them. Despite their protests, he tied our boat to theirs, ensuring that they, too, would be saved.

In that moment, relief washed over us, brief, fragile, and powerful. We were no longer alone. For the first time, the ocean felt less like a grave and more like a path to survival.

CHAPTER 20

THE RESCUE

As darkness fell, a light drizzle began, which quickly escalated into a violent storm by 9 p.m. The waves towered over our small boat, lifting it into the air and slamming it back down, sending torrents of water over us. Water had already been seeping through the hole in the soldered seam, and each crash brought more into the boat.

Fear gripped me. I clutched my mother as tightly as I could, convinced this was the end, that this storm was how we would die.

As the storm attacked us, every so often in the distance faint lights flickered. Each time we drew closer, the lights vanished. Finally, through the rain and darkness, we realized it was a Coast Guard ship. But the storm's shadows and our tiny size made us almost invisible, just a speck against the vast ocean.

In a desperate bid to signal them, my father grabbed an oar, cut the leg off his pants, wrapped it around the oar, doused it in gasoline, and set it ablaze. He waved it high, a beacon against the storm.

Thankfully, the storm had begun to ease up, the rain shifting back to a drizzle just enough for the fire to remain lit. The Coast Guard spotted us immediately. Their massive ship altered its course, heading straight toward us. Over the loudspeaker, a calm voice instructed,

"Manténganse tranquilos, sigan nuestras instrucciones, los vamos a rescatar."
"Remain calm, follow our instructions, we are going to rescue you."

As it approached, for a terrifying moment, we thought it would crush our tiny boat. At the last second, it swerved and pulled alongside us. The number 1305 was visible on its side. They continued to talk to us through the loudspeaker. They told us that we would be rescued and that they were going to bring us up one by one. They lowered a rope ladder and again instructed us that we had to come up one by one. Everyone went up as instructed with the help of my father.

In the chaos, he did not realize how close he was to the engine of our boat and he accidentally burned his leg. He was the last to board, rushing in his exhaustion, leaving everything behind, our clothes, identification, medicine, every possession that we had brought with us.

Once aboard, the guards calmly explained that they would have to shoot and sink our boat. It was standard procedure. We watched helplessly as the boat floated away, emptied of life but still holding our belongings.

Then the shots rang out, each one punctuating the loss, and the boat slowly sank into the dark sea.

Our rescue occurred around 10 p.m. that night.

At first, the Coast Guard ship had few people aboard, but as the night wore on, more refugees were brought on, and the ship became overcrowded. The bathrooms overflowed, and the carpet-like material laid on the floor for us to lay on was soon soaked. With no functioning facilities, we had no choice but to relieve ourselves where we sat.

COAST GUARD CUTTER MONHEGAN 1305, 24 AUGUST 1994
CARRYING 223 REFUGEES TO ANOTHER SHIP TO BE DROPPED OFF AT
GUANTANAMO BAY
COPYRIGHT: THE ATLANTIC
https://www.theatlantic.com/photo/2014/11/20-years-after-the-1994-cuban-raft-exodus/100852/

The ship anchored in place, and we remained aboard until the morning of Wednesday, August 24th, when we were transferred to a much larger Navy vessel. This ship was enormous, with a runway lined with planes.

Families were separated, blankets were handed out, and the vessel set sail toward Guantanamo Bay. Along the way, more refugees were picked up; the ship had to accommodate two thousand souls before reaching port. That first night, we slept on the floor where the planes were parked, the air thick with fear, exhaustion, and the smell of human waste.

Thursday was another day at sea, rescuing more people. We witnessed multiple rescues, and heartbreaking losses, watching makeshift rafts get shot and sink into the ocean. By nightfall, families with children were moved to the second floor, as the lower decks were flooded with overflowing waste. The stench, the filth, and the cramped conditions made the night unbearable.

After days of terror, exhaustion, and unimaginable loss at sea, we finally arrived at Guantanamo Bay Detention Camp around noon on Friday August 26, 1994.

CHAPTER 21

ARRIVING IN GUANTANAMO BAY

Chaos is the only word that comes close to describing our arrival at Guantanamo Bay Naval Base. Thousands of Cubans were unloaded from the ship, while military personnel rushed in every direction, shouting orders and trying to impose structure on the overwhelming flood of humanity.

I could not tell who was more confused, us or them.

At six years old, I felt frozen in place, watching the world rush past me in a blur. Everything moved fast, yet I felt stuck, suspended in time.

As soon as we were taken off the ship, we were put into two single-file lines. In front of us were two guard towers, one small and one large, marking the entrance to the camp. As we shuffled forward, each of us was handed a sack containing basic toiletries, a blanket, shorts, and a shirt.

Once everyone received their sack, we were loaded onto buses and transported to a massive tent. Inside, military guards sat behind folding tables, processing families one by one. When it was our turn, we were asked for identification. We had none. Everything we owned had been left behind on the boat that sank in the ocean. With no documents to prove who we were, they had no choice but to take us at our word, our names, and our dates of birth. Our photos were taken and placed into individual folders, which were then combined into a single-family file.

We were issued Deployable Mass Population Identification and Tracking System bracelets, known as DMPITS, each with a barcode linked to our records.

It was the only way to track such an overwhelming number of refugees. The process took hours. People kept arriving.

The lines never seemed to end.

DMPITS

After this process was completed, we were loaded back onto buses and taken to Camp Romeo. When we arrived, we were assigned to the last tent, which was already crowded with twenty-four other refugees.

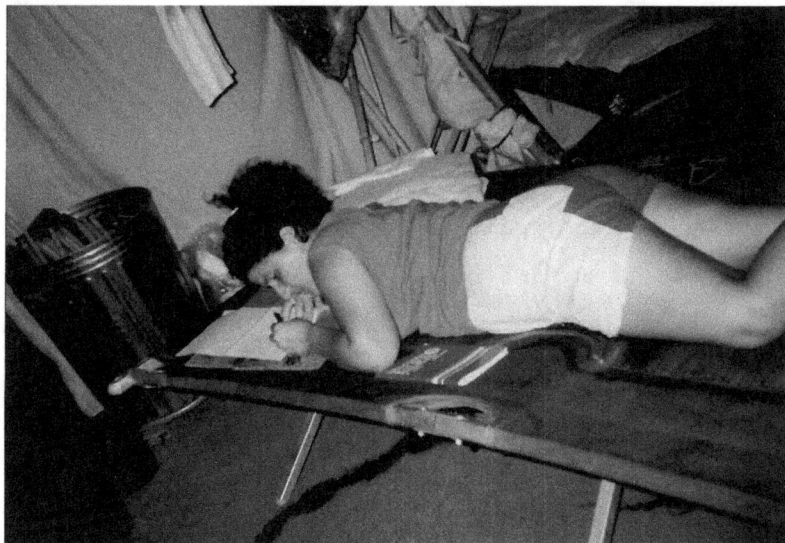

MOM WRITING LETTERS HOME ON THE COTS WE WERE GIVEN
PHOTO PROPERTY OF: CELIA E. OCHOA

Each of us were given a cot but unfortunately, with the large influx of refugee arrivals there was already a shortage of pillows and pillowcases. We received one pillow and two pillowcases.

It wasn't long before people began asking for water. Everyone was thirsty. Everyone was dehydrated. The guards told us to remain calm, that food and water would come soon. But I was in bad shape, weak, dizzy, and dangerously dehydrated.

As we settled into the tent, a truck arrived carrying a water pipe. It parked near the guard shack, and instantly, a large crowd rushed toward it. Panic erupted. People pushed, shoved, and screamed. Desperation took over.

My father and sister grabbed a bucket from our tent and went to get water for me. He told her to go ahead, she was smaller, a child, maybe she could slip through the crowd. My father could not get close. The crush of bodies was too dense. My sister tried to push forward but was shoved, slapped, and had her hair pulled. She stumbled away, crying hysterically, convinced I was going to die without water.

She sat on the ground with the empty bucket in her hands when a tall, broad-shouldered man approached her. He had already managed to get water. Seeing her cry, he asked what was wrong. Through her tears, she told him her little sister was dying and she needed water. Without hesitation, he took her bucket, handed her his own, and told her not to worry. He disappeared back into the crowd and somehow fought his way through again.

When he returned, our bucket was filled to the brim. My sister thanked him through sobs and ran back to the tent so I could drink some water.

Later that afternoon, the food truck arrived, and once again, chaos followed. People ran, pushed, and fought in desperation. Guards intervened, but injuries occurred. After that, they changed the system: each tent would designate one person to collect food for everyone.

To keep us safe, my father volunteered to go each day.

That first night was unbearable.

Using the portable bathrooms was impossible as they were overflowing with urine and feces. We squatted in corners and held our bodies in painful restraint to hold our number two. Sleeping in a tent with twenty-four strangers was terrifying. Not knowing who anyone was and what they would be capable of. The uncertainty of what tomorrow would bring or what would happen to us weighed heavy on us all.

Back in Cuba, our family had no idea whether we had survived or perished at sea. Two or three weeks into our time at Guantanamo, word spread that lists of rescued refugees that had arrived at the detention camps were being posted in Havana.

My grandfather immediately boarded a train and traveled there to search for our names. With over thirty-five thousand refugees rescued, the lists were long and the updates slow. When he checked, our names were not there. He returned home still not knowing if we were alive.

Eventually, to spare families from making the exhausting trip to Havana, Radio Martí began announcing names nightly of those who had been rescued and arrived in Guantanamo.

From that moment on, my grandmother carried her radio everywhere. She listened every single day.

One afternoon, a church member visited my grandparents and cruelly told them not to get their hopes up, claiming that thousands of body parts were washing up along the shores near Havana. He was thrown out within seconds.

My poor grandmother unraveled. She stopped eating. She stopped sleeping. She stayed glued to her radio, praying she would hear our names. One evening, my aunt Magalis came to care for her. As they listened together, my aunt fell asleep.

She was jolted awake by my grandmother screaming and crying, her voice breaking with disbelief and joy.

"¡Los escuché! ¡Los escuché con mis propios oídos! Oí cada uno de sus nombres. ¡Mi hija y mis nietas están vivas!"
"I heard them. I heard them with my own ears. Every single one of their names. My daughter and my granddaughters are alive."

For the first time in weeks, hope had finally found its way home.

CHAPTER 22

GUANTANAMO BAY - 1994

The first few months in Guantanamo were grueling. The remainder of 1994 offered no relief. Life was harsh, unpredictable, and exhausting.

We could empathize with the guards, they were clearly overwhelmed. They didn't even know exactly what to do. It quickly became obvious that confusion went both ways. We got the sense that they, too, were uncertain about what each day would bring. Unfortunately, many of the refugees were angry and hostile, which made things even more chaotic for everyone.

The first widely remembered confrontation with the guards was called the *Peanut Butter Fight*. In the early days, the only food available were yellow MRE packets, peanut butter and crackers. Instead of gratitude, frustration mounted. Some refugees began to open the peanut butter packets and smear it right on to the guards' uniforms. Others threw it right at them.

Soon, it wasn't just peanut butter. A trail between our camp and another saw guards marching daily, only to be pelted with lentil bags, an incident quickly dubbed the *Lentil Fight*. Complaints escalated with every new ration: yellow rice, then ravioli. Each time the guards tried to improve the meals, the refugees protested, throwing the food at them or refusing to eat. It was embarrassing and disheartening. Most of the guards were kind and tried their best, they were just trying to do their job and follow orders, but their efforts were met with ingratitude and hostility.

Amid the chaos, small moments of normalcy shone through.

My sister and I were invited by an Army soldier named Tina, she was Mexican and often translated for us, to attend church in the city. We sang in the choir, and for the first time, we felt a flicker of freedom and routine.

As the weeks and months passed, the constant fighting over food lost its power. The guards realized nothing would satisfy some refugees, so they stopped trying to please them. Instead, the refugees got creative. Daily rations of bread were transformed into puddings. Small fires were lit in tents to cook meals, carefully hidden from the guards as fires were forbidden. Buckets of fruit cocktail became alcohol. Laughter, songs, and makeshift celebrations followed. Hilarious drunken antics became part of camp life.

In October, we received a morale boost from Cuban-born baseball star José Canseco. He was born in Havana and had left in 1965 when he was just a year old. His family settled in Miami where he would go on to make it to major league baseball. He visited Guantanamo through his organization, Canseco's Kids. He gave out toys, and I even got to ride a bicycle in the camp.

JOSE CANSECO ARRIVING IN GUANTANAMO BAY
COPYRIGHT: CANSECO NET
https://www.canseconet.com/cuba.jpg

JOSE CANSECO PRESS CONFERENCE
COPYRIGHT: CANSECO NET
https://www.canseconet.com/speech2.jpg

After Canseco's visit, morale noticeably lifted, and for the first time, the strained relationship between the guards and the refugees began to soften and move in a more hopeful direction.

The guards taught us about Halloween and even helped us make our own costumes.

PHOTO PROPERTY OF: CELIA E. OCHOA

The guards even gave cigarettes to smokers, who quickly turned them into a form of camp currency.

My father, ever the strategist, would bet packs of cigarettes on my pool skills, confident that I could beat any grown man. They always laughed at him, confident that they could not lose to a seven-year-old. Boy were they wrong and my father ended up with more packs than anyone else in the entire camp.

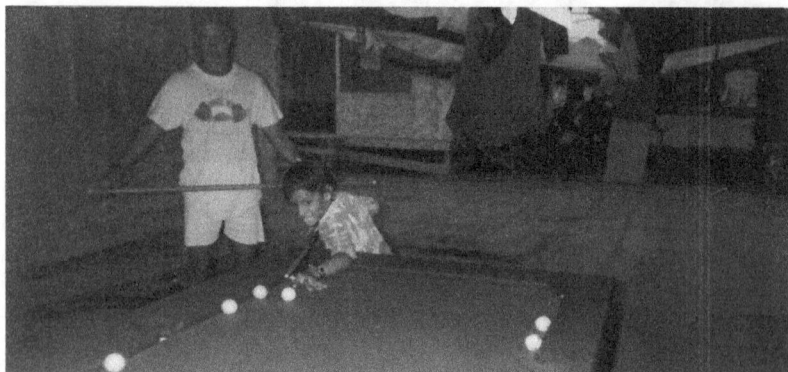

PLAYING FOR CIGARETTES @ CAMP VILLA LIMA
PHOTO PROPERTY OF: CELIA E. OCHOA

Later, Cuban singer Willy Chirino visited, performing at every camp. Then he came to ours and my sister and I attended the concert. For a few hours, music replaced fear and monotony.

WILLY CHIRINO. GUANTANAMO 1994. FACEBOOK, 13 SEPTEMBER 2014
https://www.facebook.com/willychirino/photos/

WILLY CHIRINO. GUANTANAMO 1994. FACEBOOK, 13 SEPTEMBER 2014
https://www.facebook.com/willychirino/photos/

Once again, our spirits were lifted.

Then, nature reminded us of who was really in charge. On November 12th, a tropical storm hit. Guards scrambled to secure the tents, but the ropes never made it to us in time. The pile of ropes sat under their guard tower.

Winds reached 120 miles per hour and our tent started to lift off the ground, ultimately tearing one of the tent's ropes. The guards would not leave their tower to help or even to give us the ropes. My father begged for help as he tried to hold onto the snapped rope.

He noticed that the wind was also slightly lifting the barbed wire from the ground and he took that opportunity, ignoring the guards' protests, and he crawled under the wires to grab a rope from under the guard tower.

Despite being cut by the wires, he retrieved a rope, crawled back under and secured our tent. Soaked and shivering, we survived the night thanks to his actions.

In the early hours of November 13th, 1994, Hurricane Gordon hit Guantanamo Bay Naval Base.

Storms Hits Guantanamo

🎁 Give this article ↪ 🔖

By The Associated Press
Nov. 14, 1994

The New York Times Archives

About the Archive
This is a digitized version of an article from The Times's print archive, before the start of online publication in 1996. To preserve these articles as they originally appeared, The Times does not alter, edit or update them.

Occasionally the digitization process introduces transcription errors or other problems; we are continuing to work to improve these archived versions.

Tropical Storm Gordon hit the Cuban and Haitian refugee camps in Guantanamo Bay, Cuba, today with gusts of wind up to 120 miles per hour.

The storm toppled tents but otherwise caused little damage at the American Navy base housing thousands of refugees.

No serious injuries were reported among 23,000 Cubans and 6,000 Haitians being held at Guantanamo Bay, where about 7 inches of rain fell overnight.

THE NEW YORK TIMES ARCHIVE
https://www.nytimes.com/1994/11/14/world/storms-hits-guantanamo.html

Around five that morning, as the water rose and the camp began to flood, guards rushed through, ordering us to pack whatever we could fit into our sacks. There was no time to gather belongings carefully, only to move. We were quickly loaded onto buses and taken to Camp McCalla 5.

That camp sat on higher ground and had avoided the flooding, but any sense of relief vanished almost immediately. The tents were infested with worms, making them impossible to enter. In that camp, many refugees had resorted to relieving themselves inside the tents rather than walking to the portable bathrooms. The stench was overwhelming. Complaints erupted, and the guards, clearly overwhelmed themselves, told us to wait while they tried to decide where to send us next.

Eventually, we were transported once more, this time to a dome-shaped warehouse meant to shelter us from the hurricane. We sat on the hard floor all night long, waiting as the storm raged outside and uncertainty settled in. It wasn't until the following morning that we were taken to McCalla 4. Upon arrival, we were told that this camp would be our home for the time being.

McCalla 4 was also where we were first given access to the beach, a small but powerful comfort after days of fear, exhaustion, and displacement.

MOM AND I AT THE BEACH @ CAMP McCALLA 4
PHOTO PROPERTY OF: CELIA E. OCHOA

AT THE BEACH @ CAMP McCALLA 4
PHOTO PROPERTY OF: CELIA E. OCHOA

By the time Christmas arrived, the guards made a visible effort to bring a sense of joy into the camp. Large speakers were set up at the entrance, filling the air with music throughout the day. We were given what we considered a *'nicer'* meal than usual, the most coveted HDRs, Humanitarian Daily Rations. That Christmas also marked a small but unforgettable first: the day we tasted a Twinkie for the very first time.

CHAPTER 23

GUANTANAMO BAY - 1995

By the new year, things were getting better, and everything had fallen into a routine. In their efforts to improve the conditions in the camps, the guards and the refugees came to a mutual understanding that it would benefit all to work together.

Those that were teachers, doctors, sports players, artists, dancers, and musicians were asked to help. Teachers started having classes for children and adults. Doctors assisted military doctors. Sports players put together teams and started hosting games. Artists held drawing classes and painting sessions. Dancers put together dance teams and would hold dance classes. Musicians were provided with instruments and held classes to teach how to play them. All of these efforts absolutely improved the relationship between the guards and refugees.

As there were many teachers at the camps, a school in Spanish was eventually opened, which my sister and I attended. I had not had the opportunity to attend school up until this point and it was all very new and exciting.

Eventually, Navy Seabees came in to build a park for us kids. Once the park was completed, activities were held there, and it became one of my absolute favorite places to go. This is where I heard for the first time the music of Ace of Base. Their 1993 album was a favorite among the guards and as such it was played from start to finish on many occasions. I didn't understand what they sang about, and I didn't speak any English, but I sang every word of every song.

From that point forward, every night we had something to look forward to. Games of bingo and dominoes, comedy shows and social events.

The guards continued trying to make our stay better. But no matter what they did there were many Cubans that no matter how much the camp conditions improved, they were still going out of their mind and just wanted to get out of the camps. People started to be moved to camps in Panama. And many wanted to volunteer to go as they were under the impression that if you went to Panama, you would be able to go to the United States. But that didn't happen, in fact, some were even transferred right back to Guantanamo.

This was about the time that many started to attempt, and some even succeeded in committing suicide. There was no restricted access to things like in a traditional prison. Ropes, knives, toxic products, everything was within reach. The attempts and successes ranged from hanging to slit wrists to digesting toxic chemicals. Some managed to escape back to unoccupied Cuba. To do this was almost as risky as it was when we all escaped. To make it back they had to scale the barbed wire, climb down a forty-foot cliff and swim about a mile to Cuban territory. The desperation was evident.

Between the military base and the rest of Cuba there were mines. Many attempted to escape by passing through them. Daily, we would hear explosions coming from the direction of the mines. Many died from those explosions. Others survived but after being medically treated, they were returned to camp missing limbs. Some without a leg, others without an arm.

As talks began of releasing detainees to the United States, they started to prioritize who would be released first. They began with older people, followed by adults and children with medical issues.

One day, while walking along the edge of the camp, I stopped to look at posters hanging from the barbed wire. The images burned themselves into my memory: a man's leg sliced open from knee to ankle, infection clearly visible; severely burned body parts; another man with his stomach cut open. Across each poster, in large bold letters, were the words:

"Esto no te llevará a los Estados Unidos."
This will not get you to the United States.

These posters were warnings, showing what not to do in hopes of gaining parole. That was when I truly understood how desperate people had become.

The images depicted what single men were doing to themselves to be classified as having *'medical issues.'* Some cut open their legs and packed the wounds with dirt to cause infections, believing it would require treatment unavailable in the camps and force their transfer to the U.S.

Some lost limbs and still were not sent to the United States. Instead, they were returned to Cuba.

Others melted the plastic from HDR meal packets and poured it onto their arms, legs, and bodies, intentionally causing severe third-degree burns.

Some hoarded the powdered chocolate packets from their meals, eating ten, twenty, even thirty at once to induce extreme diarrhea, dehydration, and hemorrhoids. If that didn't work, they took blankets and tied knots and would insert them in their rear end, yanking it as hard as they could to deliberately cause the hemorrhoids and injure themselves further.

One man cut his stomach open, certain he would be evacuated for medical care. By then, however, there were enough doctors on base to treat him. They stitched him up and sent him right back to camp.

So much desperation.

My father eventually sat us down and asked what we were going to do to get out. Many families with children had already been granted passage, and he felt we needed to do something to help our chances.

My sister Evelyn was unraveling. She cried constantly, longing for our family and our home. At times, she went days without speaking. When beach access was allowed, she would sit by the water for hours, crying. Eventually, the decision was made to take her to see a doctor.

She wouldn't speak during the appointment, only cried. When she finally did talk, she was diagnosed with depression and deemed in need of mental health services. She was transferred to a psychiatric ward, where she was the only child.

She later described it as a prison. Every day began at 4 a.m. with forced running, followed by group activities, and ended with one-on-one sessions with a doctor.

One morning, she refused to get up. A staff member she trusted told her,

"Ochoa, tienes que levantarte o te ponen una camisa de fuerza y te llevan a un calabozo."
Ochoa, you have to get up or they'll put you in a straitjacket and take you to a cell.

By then, she was too traumatized to care. Just two days earlier, she had woken up to find her roommate had hung herself with bed sheets. Evelyn had been crying nonstop ever since and couldn't bring herself to get out of bed.

Five soldiers came in, then two more. She kicked and screamed, making it impossible to restrain her, which made it impossible to get the straitjacket on her. Eventually, they sprayed her with a hose to calm her down. Afterward, the same staff member returned, speaking gently, asking why she had reacted that way, and begging her not to do it again.

After that, she never resisted again. She kept her head down and followed every rule. All she wanted was to leave and be back with us.

The hospital was far from the camps, and we were only allowed to visit her twice during her stay. She remained there for about two months.

At her final appointment, the doctor told us he was granting our family parole due to Evelyn's mental health condition. She could leave the hospital. It had finally happened; we were approved to go to the United States. Evelyn was asked to list who would accompany her. She named our parents, me, and Roli, who she listed as my godfather.

Two days later, we were told to prepare to leave. On June 7, 1995, we were taken out of Camp Villa Lima. On June 8, 1995, we boarded a flight to the United States.

7 JUNE 1995 CAMP VILLA LIMA
PHOTO PROPERTY OF: CELIA E. OCHOA

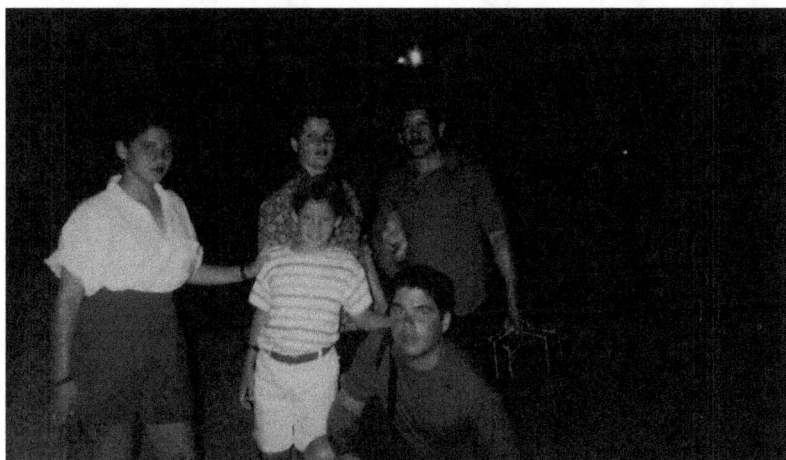

8 JUNE 1995 BEFORE BOARDING OUR FLIGHT TO THE U.S.
PHOTO PROPERTY OF: CELIA E. OCHOA

8 JUNE 1995 BOARDING OUR FLIGHT TO THE U.S.
PHOTO PROPERTY OF: CELIA E. OCHOA

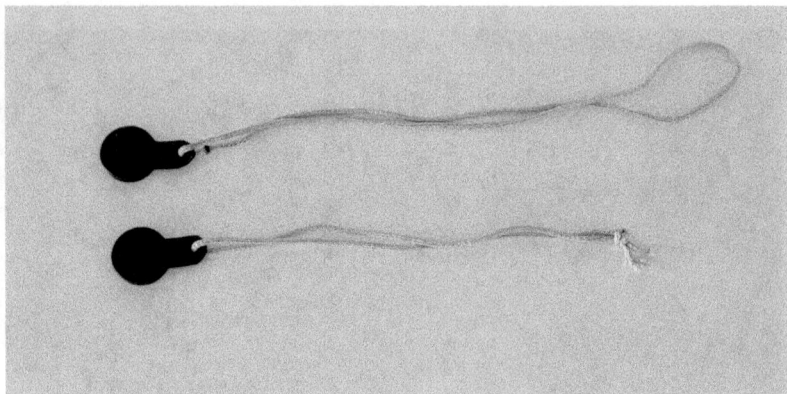

OUR DIMPITS CONVERTED TO NECKLACES BY THE GUARDS WHEN WE LEFT GUANTANAMO
PHOTO PROPERTY OF: CELIA E. OCHOA

CHAPTER 24

ARRIVING IN THE UNITED STATES

From Guantánamo, we were flown to Miami, Florida.

The moment we got off the plane, we were escorted directly to an immigration office, where we spent the rest of the day completing paperwork. We had no identification of any kind, so everything had to be processed from scratch.

We were told that, through our sponsorship, we could be resettled in one of three places:

- Louisville, Kentucky
- Houston, Texas
- Ithaca, New York

We had no idea where any of them were, but for reasons I still can't fully explain, my parents chose Ithaca.

During the process, a woman from the church that had sponsored us entered the room and introduced herself. She explained that she would be responsible for taking us to our hotel. When we arrived, we were given written instructions in Spanish explaining the rules and expectations for our stay.

Roli had a brother living in Miami, so he went to stay with him instead of staying at the hotel. The following day, they returned to pick us up so we could visit his brother's home. We were in awe the moment we stepped inside. To us, it felt like a mansion, something far beyond anything we had ever seen or imagined.

Their daughter took Evelyn and me to her bedroom and began offering us some of her belongings. We were overwhelmed. We had never seen so many toys, never seen a bedroom like that in our lives.

Afterward, we returned to the hotel. The next day, the church representative picked us up again so we could complete even more paperwork. We stayed in Miami until our identification was issued and our parents received their work authorization documents. On June 14, they were finally approved. The very next day, we were taken back to the airport to begin the final leg of our journey to Ithaca, New York.

INSTRUCTIONS FOR OUR HOTEL STAY
PHOTO PROPERTY OF: CELIA E. OCHOA

INSTRUCTIONS FOR REFUGEES

WELCOME TO MIAMI, FLORIDA. USES. "LAND OF FREEDOM"

* *

THE FOLLOWING STANDARDS ARE REQUIRED AT THE HOTEL WHERE THEY

ARE STAYING.

1st.- ONLY ONE ROOM KEY WILL BE PROVIDED.

2nd.-THE KEY MUST BE RETURNED TO THE HOTEL FOLDER

WHEN ABSENT FOR ANY REASON.

TEMPORARY ABSENCE

WHEN YOU ARE TEMPORARILY ABSENT FOR ANY REASON, YOU MUST

INFORM THE HOTEL FOLDER THE TELEPHONE OR ADDRESS WHERE

YOU WILL BE. YOU SHOULD ALWAYS BE REACHABLE.

DEFINITIVE ABSENCE

IF YOU ARE PERMANENTLY ABSENT FROM THE HOTEL WITH ANY FAMILY

MEMBER WHO GUARANTEES YOU TO BE YOUR SPONSOR, YOU SHOULD

IMMEDIATELY CONTACT ANGEL GONZALEZ'S BIPPER TELEPHONE THROUGH

THE HOTEL FOLDER.

YOU HAVE THE DUTY TO INFORM YOUR NEW ADDRESS WHERE C WILL RESIDE

YOUR FAMILY MEMBER OR SPONSOR AND BE SO LOCATED FOR US TO

ADDRESS YOUR CASE EFFICIENTLY.

THANK YOU VERY MUCH FOR YOUR COOPERATION TO

THE BETTER OPERATION OF OUR ORGANIZATION!!!

IMPORTANT!!! VISITS ARE PROHIBITED IN THE ROOM. AND

THE TELEPHONE CALLS WILL BE FROM THE HOTEL OFFICE:

CALLS: 3 DAILY CALLS FOR NO MORE THAN 3 MINUTES.

DOCUMENT TRANSLATED TO ENGLISH
PHOTO PROPERTY OF: CELIA E. OCHOA

CHAPTER 25

LIFE AFTER GUANTANAMO BAY

Life after the Guantánamo Bay detention camps was never easy. Our family struggled through those early years in the United States, and the tragic life we had known in Cacocum did not stay behind. In many ways, it followed us.

Ithaca, NY (1995 – 2000)

We were fortunate to arrive through a refugee sponsorship program called *Church World Service.*

REFUGEE RESETTLEMENT PROGRAM PAPERWORK
PHOTO PROPERTY OF: CELIA E. OCHOA

Through the generosity of church members, everything was initially provided for us, hotel accommodations, flights, and even housing. One woman from the church opened her home to us and offered to foster our family while we completed our paperwork and until my parents could find work and we could secure a place of our own. Her name was LeGrace, one of the kindest, most remarkable human beings we have ever known. We lived with her from June through August of 1995, and her compassion left a lasting mark on our lives.

WHERE WE LIVED
COPYRIGHT: MELANIE COLTER
https://pocketsights.com/tours/place/

ON THE PORCH
PHOTO PROPERTY OF: CELIA E. OCHOA

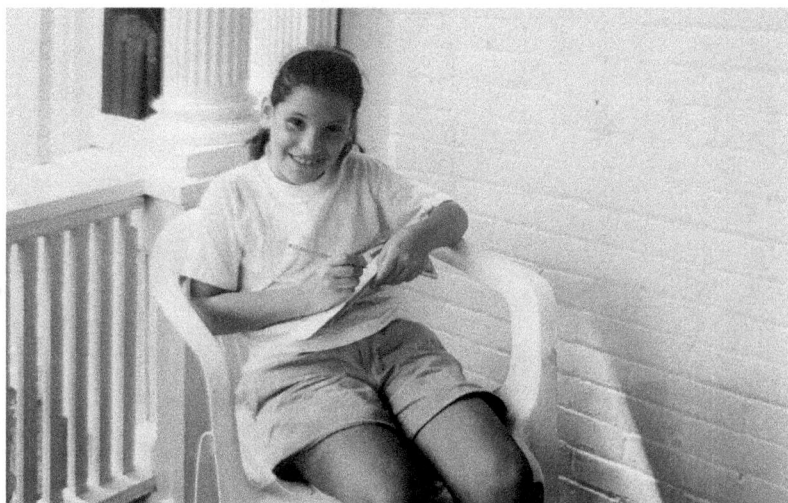

WRITING ON THE PORCH
PHOTO PROPERTY OF: CELIA E. OCHOA

Once our documents were finalized and my parent's found jobs, we qualified for housing assistance.

MOVING INTO OUR OWN PLACE
PHOTO PROPERTY OF: CELIA E. OCHOA

OUR FIRST SNOW
PHOTO PROPERTY OF: CELIA E. OCHOA

In 1996, my aunt Magalis, who had tried to escape with us back in 1993, won the Cuban lottery. Winning meant that she and her family could legally leave Cuba if they paid for the paperwork and airfare themselves. From 1996 to 1999, we lived right next door to her family. We were at 218; they were at 222.

218 AND 222
COPYRIGHT: GOOGLE MAPS

Life in Ithaca, in many ways, mirrored life in Cacocum.

We had escaped communism. We had escaped being permanently targeted for our last name. We had survived a literal prison camp. But you can never truly escape who you are, and despite being in a new country, my father remained the same man he had always been.

Every weekend, he found a reason to throw a party. And every weekend ended in drunken chaos. Police visits. Arrests. Blood, far too much blood.

It is painful to admit, but that is what I associate most with Ithaca. Weekend after weekend, that was my reality. Sometimes it was my sister's blood, after my father violently ripped earrings from her ears. Other times it was his own blood from punching holes through walls, from shattered beer bottles smashed against his forehead. By Monday mornings, neighbors would notice droplets of blood on the sidewalk and mutter, *"The Ochoa's must have had another party."* Sadly, they were never wrong.

One memory stands above all others. At my tenth birthday party, my father wanted to leave and drive drunk. When no one gave him his keys, he became enraged. To intimidate everyone into handing them over, he grabbed a knife. What he didn't realize was that I had the keys.

I was just about to run upstairs and hide them when he saw them in my hand.

Suddenly, I was running, and he was chasing me, knife in hand.

To this day, I don't think I have ever run faster. I reached my bedroom, slammed the door shut, and locked it. Seconds later, a hand crashed through the center of the door.

That image is forever burned into my mind, like a scene straight out of The Shining.

Orlando, FL (2000 – 2014)

In the summer of 1999, my uncle Roget visited a friend in Florida and almost immediately decided to move his family there. Within months, they packed up and relocated to Orlando.

That Christmas, we visited them in their new home, and by January of 2000, we followed in their footsteps and made our way to Orlando.

LOADING UP TO HEAD TO ORLANDO
PHOTO COPYRIGHT OF: CELIA E. OCHOA

It was supposed to be another fresh start. But by then, history had already taught us the truth: changing our location never changed the outcome. It only changed where the chaos unfolded. The abuse continued.

At eleven years old, I felt helpless watching my mother and sister suffer and eventually, even my newborn niece. I remember the heartbreak of seeing my sister and her baby thrown out onto the streets for no reason at all, forced to live in a Ronald McDonald House.

Not even his own granddaughter was enough to make my father want to change.

In August of 2000, we bought our first home. Another move. Another promise of a new beginning.

OUR FIRST HOME IN ORLANDO
COPYRIGHT: ZILLOW HOMES

Once again, there was no new beginning like he promised. Nothing changed, except me.

I had always been quiet and reserved, careful not to provoke him. For a long time, that strategy worked. He mostly left me alone. I should have known it couldn't last forever.

About a month after moving in, he forbade me from being friends with a girl who lived down the street. He claimed she was a bad influence. The truth was much darker: he had been having an affair with her mother. He believed my friend might have seen him sneaking into her house at night and feared she would tell me.

Because we walked in the same direction after getting off the school bus, we occasionally ended up near each other on the sidewalk, even without speaking. One afternoon, he drove by and saw us close enough to assume we were talking, even though we had not uttered a single word to each other.

When I reached our house, he ripped the keys from my hand, screamed at me for disobeying him, went inside, and locked me out. I spent hours sitting in the carport, pounding on the door and crying,

"Papi, por favor déjame entrar."
"Daddy, please let me in."

Two hours later, my mother came home from work and found me, on the floor in the carport, sobbing. When I told her what had happened, something in her finally broke. That night, she and I slept in her van.

MOM'S VAN THAT WE SLEPT IN
PHOTO PROPERTY OF: CELIA E. OCHOA

The next day, we returned, because we had nowhere else to go. That first night back, my mother moved into my room.

Within days, she had secured an apartment. On December 18th, the day her job began their year-end shut down, we packed what he allowed us to take and left.

It was one of the best days of my life.

From that moment on, my mother worked relentlessly to build a life without him. She was dependable, driven, and resilient, and it was no surprise how quickly she excelled at work. She made sure we were always taken care of.

I am forever grateful for the choice she made that day and endlessly proud of the woman she became.

I know, without a doubt, that I would not be who I am today without her.

I graduated high school and became the first in my family to attend college. I earned a bachelor's degree in criminal justice and investigations. In the months leading up to graduation, I applied for every entry-level position I could find, only to be turned away repeatedly. Most required years of experience. Those that didn't, gave preference to veterans. Every opening had at least one veteran applicant.

That reality led me to a decision that would change my life: joining the United States Navy. The friendships I had formed with guards at Guantánamo had stayed with me. They inspired my four years in JROTC and planted a seed I had carried for a long time. At that point in my life, it felt like the right moment.

But life has a way of complicating even the best-timed decisions.

JUNE 26, 4:05 PM

Hey aren't you ███████'s best friend?

Twenty-two days after signing my enlistment papers, the unexpected happened.

I wasn't scheduled to leave for boot camp for another eight months. Getting involved with anyone made no sense. So instead, we talked about staying friends. We made a bucket list of things we wanted to do before I left and decided we'd do them together. And when I say we tried to remain just friends, we truly tried. But some things are impossible to deny. Eventually, we gave in. For those eight months, we packed in as many memories as we could, knowing there was an end date looming. A love I never expected to find had found me, and I was preparing to leave it behind.

Great Lakes, Illinois (2014)

In February 2014, I left for eight weeks of boot camp.

That April, I graduated as a United States Navy Sailor, one of the proudest moments of my life.

PHOTO PROPERTY OF: CELIA E. OCHOA

Because I was deploying almost immediately, we didn't wait. On May 30th, I married my best friend.

It was a simple courthouse ceremony, just the two of us, no family, no friends. The timing wasn't ideal, but it was right. In 2015, we made up for it with the wedding of our dreams back home in Orlando, surrounded by our children, our families, and the friends who had carried us through every chapter.

We were stationed in Norfolk, Virginia until I accepted a civilian position in Jacksonville, Florida and separated from active duty. Jacksonville became home.

In the years since, we went on to purchase three beautiful homes, each one an upgrade to make room for our ever-growing family. In 2019, we became foster parents, a journey that was as challenging as it was rewarding. It brought joy and heartbreak, tears and laughter. It broke us open and stitched us back together again. That journey led us to the adoption of our two beautiful baby girls. And in the end, every hard moment, every uncertain step, every emotional turn was worth it.

Unfortunately, after eleven and a half years together and ten years of marriage, life took us in a different direction, and our journey together came to an end in December of 2024 when our divorce was finalized. The last few years of the marriage slowly drained life out of me. What once felt like partnership turned into survival.

I was exhausted in ways rest could not repair, emotionally, mentally, and spiritually. I was carrying the weight of holding everything together while quietly losing pieces of myself. Staying began to cost me not only my peace, but my ability to be the parent my children deserved.

Making the decision to file for divorce was one of the hardest choices I ever had to make, but it was also the most necessary. It wasn't just the best decision for me; it was the best decision for my kids. Choosing to leave meant choosing a healthier, calmer environment for them. It meant showing them that love should not feel heavy, that safety and peace matter, and that it is okay to walk away from something that no longer nurtures you.

Life since then has been lighter. I can breathe again. I am more present, more patient, and more emotionally available for my children. I have rediscovered joy, stability, and parts of myself I didn't realize I had buried. Most unexpectedly, I also found love again. A love that is healthy, uplifting, and full of partnership and respect. The pain of that chapter shaped me, but it no longer defines our lives.

Sometimes love doesn't last forever, and sometimes, letting go is the bravest and most loving thing you can do, not just for yourself, but for your children too. And sometimes, letting go, opens the door to finding love again.

CHAPTER 26

MY FINAL THOUGHTS

At seven years old, I promised myself that I would never squander the opportunity I had been given by making it to this country. And today, at thirty-seven, I look back with pride at everything I have accomplished. I was the first in my family to graduate high school, the first to attend college. I worked while going to school full-time. I joined the United States Navy. And I have built a beautiful life with my children.

No one, not even me, could have imagined that the same little girl held by the United States military in the Guantánamo Bay Detention Camps would grow up to serve in the United States military herself. I suppose that is the true irony of life.

To say I've been through a lot would be an understatement. I've literally died, survived eighteen hours in the ocean, endured ten months in a detention camp, lived under an abusive father, and faced significant hatred for being queer. I've chosen not to dive deeply into the complicated journey of discovering myself and coming out, it could easily fill a book of its own. But I have been out for more than half of my life, twenty years, and while some things have changed, in many ways, it still feels like they haven't. To be judged for who you love rather than who you are fundamentally at your core is a sad reality.

I grew up in the Seventh Day Adventist Church, and though I stepped away from organized religion years ago, I carried one lasting lesson with me: being a good human being is the most important thing you can do with your time on this Earth. Being gay does not erase the good I have done or continue to do.

We often take daily life for granted, but some experiences leave permanent imprints. These experiences remind us of how much we have to be grateful for. For me, one of those moments is the night we drifted farther and farther from Cuba, the only home I had ever known. It is a constant reminder of how lucky I am to be where I am today. Now, whenever I feel myself taking something for granted, I think of that night. A night, a day, a moment, a memory, an experience etched into my memory that keeps gratitude at the forefront of my life.

The bullies of my early years never knew the fire they would ignite in seven-year-old me. Thanks to them, no matter what life throws my way, I have an internal voice that will always guide me, telling me:

"ROW YOUR BOAT CUBAN REFUGEE"

THE END

AUTHORS NOTE
PART 2

Throughout the rest of this book, you will come across a collection of photographs dating from August 1994 to June 1995, capturing our time in the Guantánamo Bay Detention Camps.

Most of these images feature myself and my family during that period. However, there are also photos of others, people we left Cuba with, individuals we met in the camps, and even some of the guards who showed us kindness. For some, we know only a first name or a last name. For others, all that remains are these photographs, with no identifying information at all.

I fully understand that the chances may be slim, but my greatest hope for this memoir is that someone featured in these photographs will come across it. I dream of the possibility of reconnecting with those people after almost thirty-two years. Just imagining someone from that time seeing themselves in these pages and reaching out fills me with indescribable emotion. That is why I am not only profoundly grateful that we were able to salvage these photographs but also deeply honored to include them here.

Social media has incredible reach and power, and I hope it will help this book find the people in these photographs.

On behalf of myself and my family, I want to sincerely thank you, not just for reading this story, but for any posts, shares, or efforts that might help us reconnect with those featured in the pages to follow.

Thank you, from the bottom of our hearts.

Love,

CELIA E. OCHOA

PHOTOGRAPHS

GUANTANAMO BAY, CUBA 1994-1995

EVERYONE FROM OUR BOAT
DATE: 18 OCTOBER 1994 CAMP: ROMEO
PHOTO PROPERTY OF: CELIA E. OCHOA

PHOTO PROPERTY OF: CELIA E. OCHOA

TAKING A BATH IN CAMP VILLA LIMA CABIN: B-13
PHOTO PROPERTY OF: CELIA E. OCHOA

PHOTO PROPERTY OF: CELIA E. OCHOA

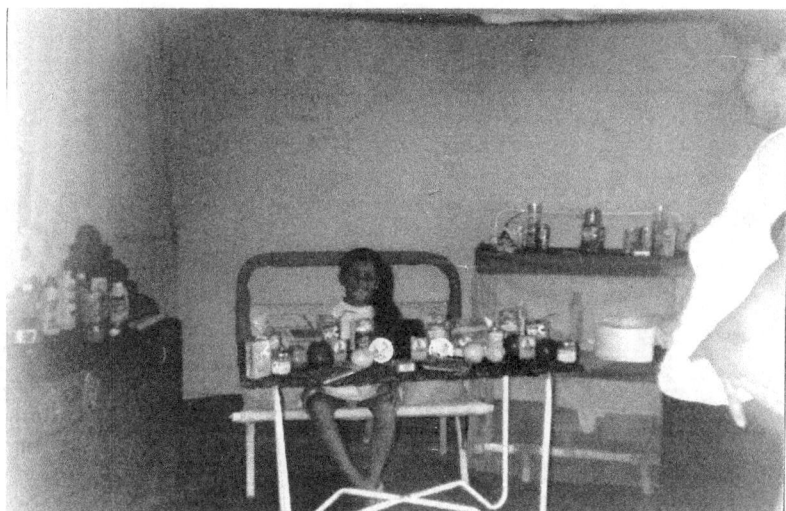

ME AND MY MOM
PHOTO PROPERTY OF: CELIA E. OCHOA

EVELYN, IDALMIS (MOM) AND ME
PHOTO PROPERTY OF: CELIA E. OCHOA

PHOTO PROPERTY OF: CELIA E. OCHOA

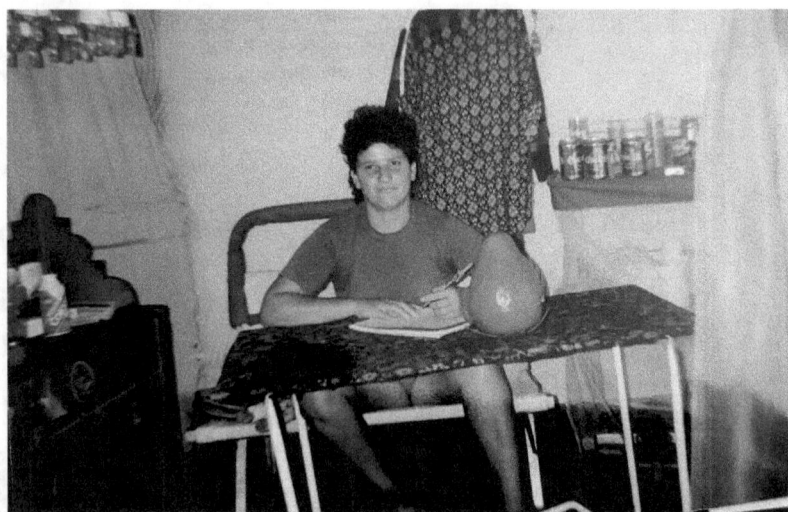

PHOTO PROPERTY OF: CELIA E. OCHOA

CAMP: McCALLA 4
PHOTO PROPERTY OF: CELIA E. OCHOA

PHOTO PROPERTY OF: CELIA E. OCHOA

CAMP: McCALLA 4
PHOTO PROPERTY OF: CELIA E. OCHOA

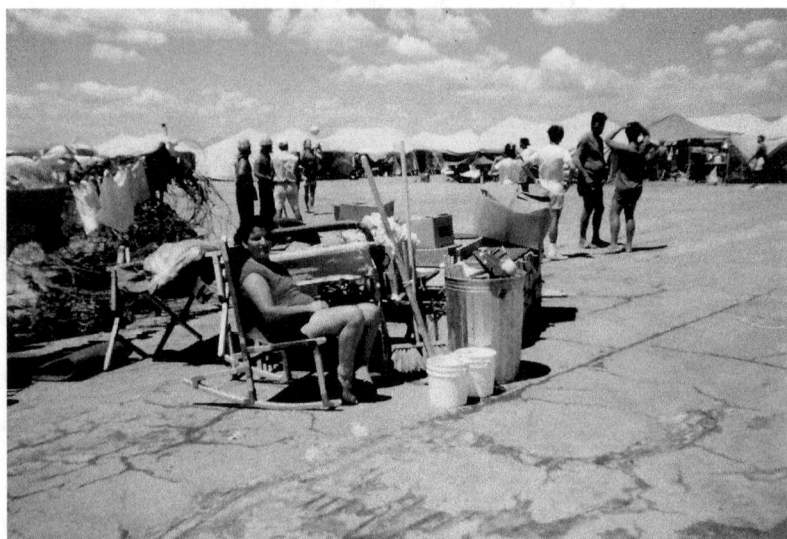

PHOTO PROPERTY OF: CELIA E. OCHOA

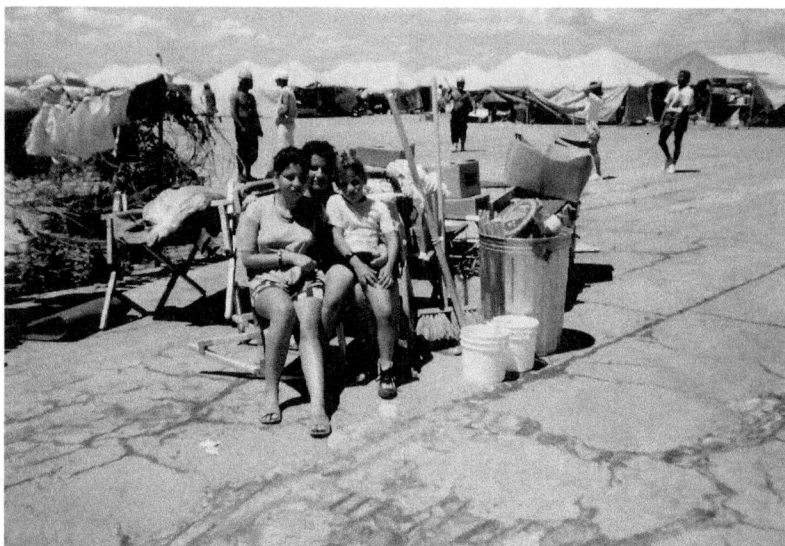

CAMP TRANSFER CAMP: McCALLA 4
PHOTO PROPERTY OF: CELIA E. OCHOA

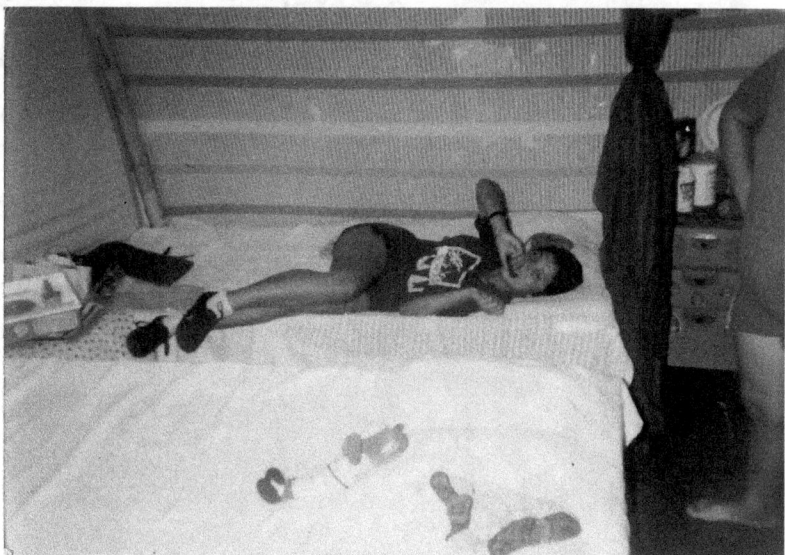

PHOTO PROPERTY OF: CELIA E. OCHOA

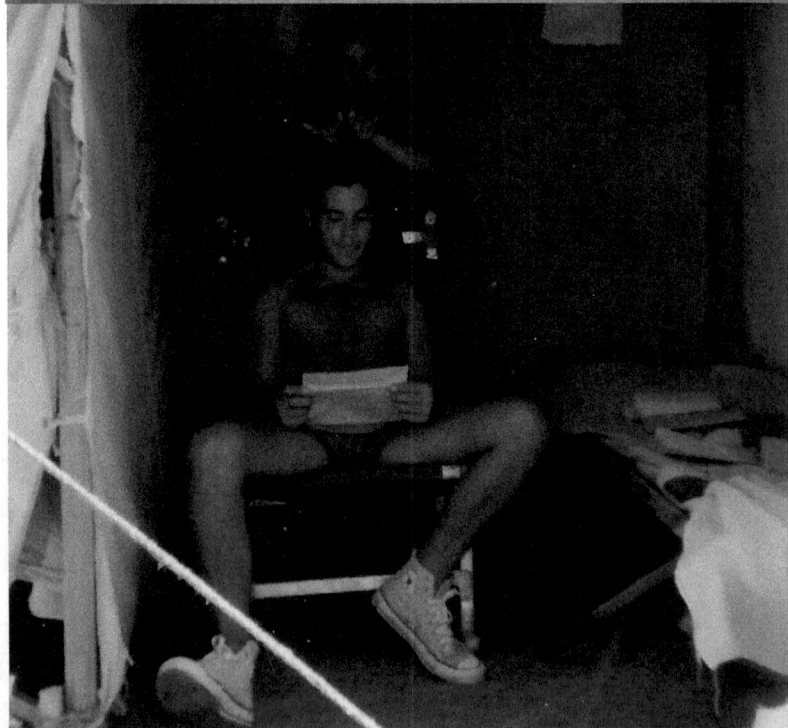

EVELYN AND OSBALDO
PHOTO PROPERTY OF: CELIA E. OCHOA

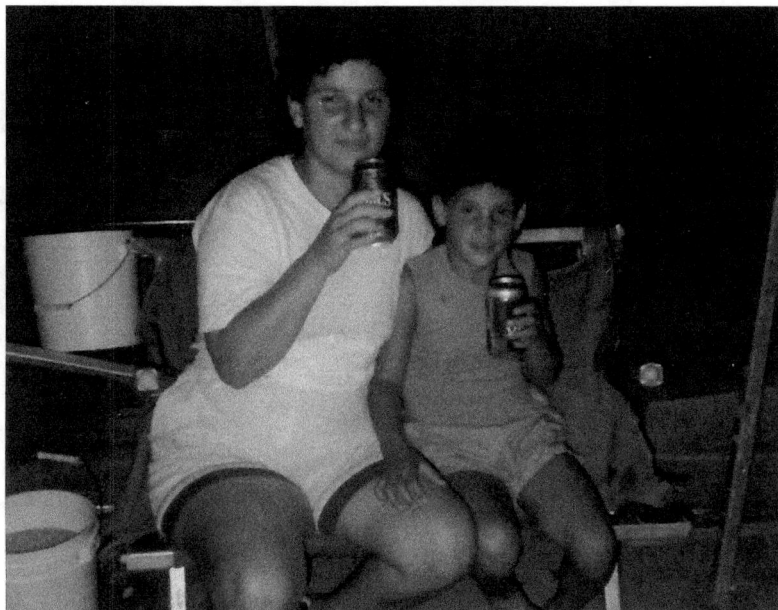

MOM AND ME
PHOTO PROPERTY OF: CELIA E. OCHOA

1 MAY 1995 - MY 7TH BIRTHDAY
PHOTO PROPERTY OF: CELIA E. OCHOA

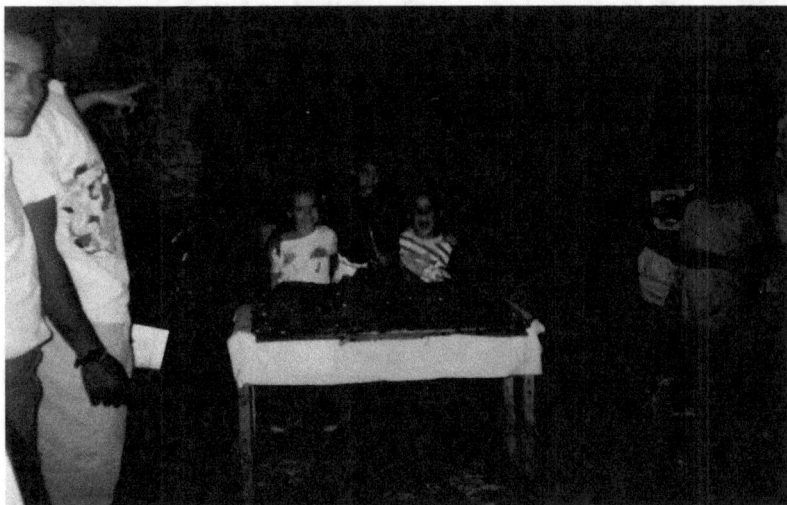

1 MAY 1995 - MY 7TH BIRTHDAY
PHOTO PROPERTY OF: CELIA E. OCHOA

ME AND MAYLIN PEREZ DIAZ
PHOTO PROPERTY OF: CELIA E. OCHOA

DAYLIN DIAZ AND EVELYN
PHOTO PROPERTY OF: CELIA E. OCHOA

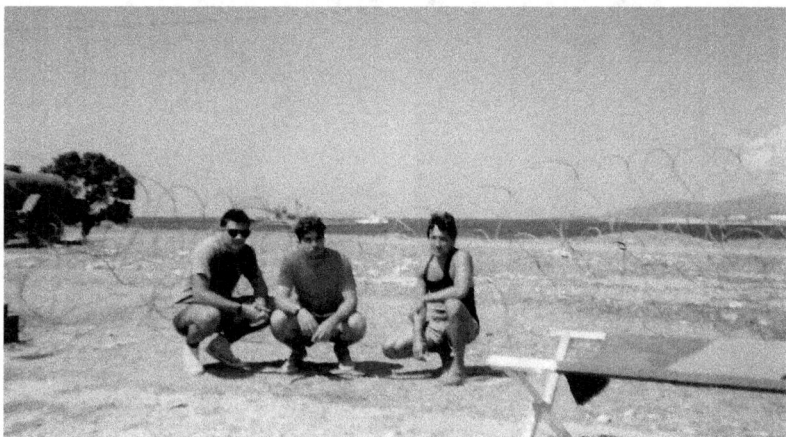

JORDI, ROLI AND MY FATHER
PHOTO PROPERTY OF: CELIA E. OCHOA

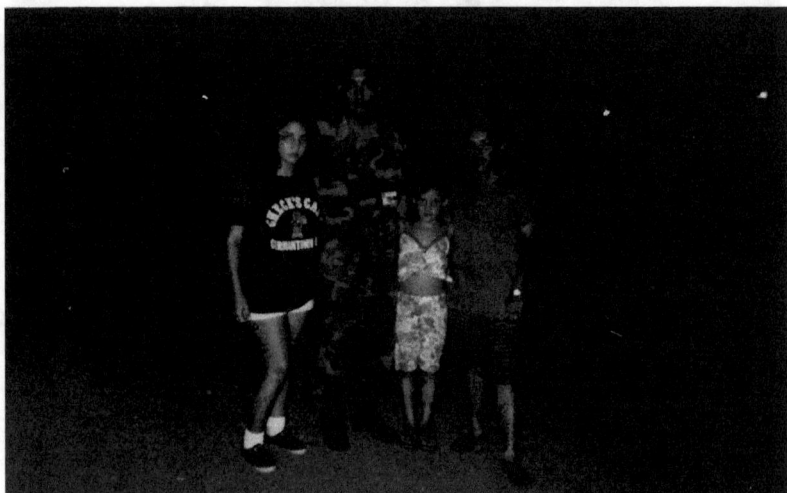

EVELYN, ARMY SOLDIER ORTEGA AND UNKNOWN MAN
PHOTO PROPERTY OF: CELIA E. OCHOA

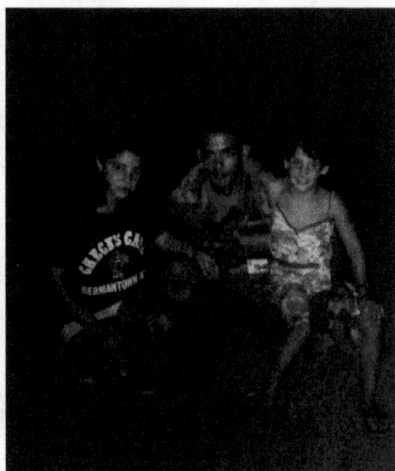

EVELYN AND ME WITH ARMY SOLDIER ORTEGA
PHOTO PROPERTY OF: CELIA E. OCHOA

PHOTO PROPERTY OF: CELIA E. OCHOA

WOMAN FROM HUMANITARIAN VISITS
PHOTO PROPERTY OF: CELIA E. OCHOA

PHOTO PROPERTY OF: CELIA E. OCHOA

PHOTO PROPERTY OF: CELIA E. OCHOA

ARMY SOLDIER LAST NAME PARK GIFTED ME THIS PHOTO OF HIM
PHOTO PROPERTY OF: CELIA E. OCHOA

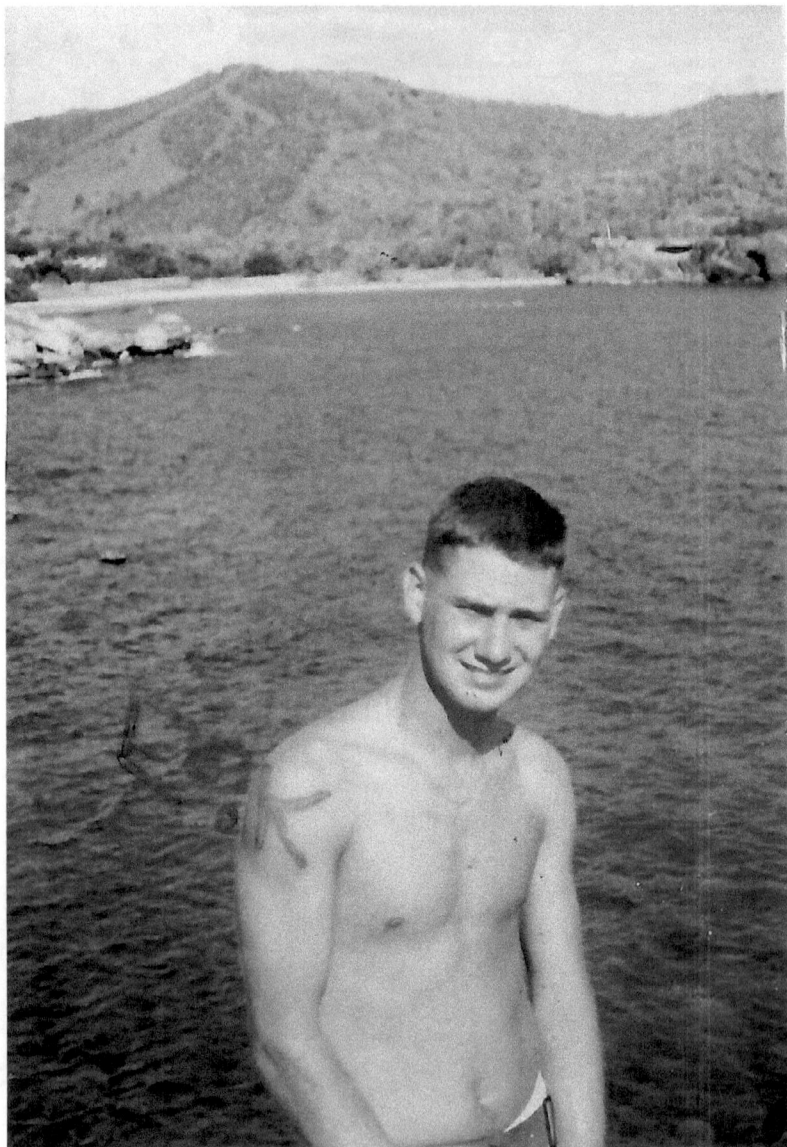

ARMY SOLDIER ERIK EDWARDS RODRIGUEZ
PHOTO PROPERTY OF: CELIA E. OCHOA

ME WITH BASE GUARDS
PHOTO PROPERTY OF: CELIA E. OCHOA

EVELYN AND ARMY SOLDIER HILLIS
PHOTO PROPERTY OF: CELIA E. OCHOA

ARMY SOLDIER COHEN
PHOTO PROPERTY OF: CELIA E. OCHOA

DESCRIPTION: CUBAN MIGRANTS WALK TO A US NAVY LANDING
CRAFT THAT WILL FERRY THEM ACROSS GUANTANAMO BAY,
ENROUTE TO THEIR PAROLE FLIGHT FROM THE US NAVAL BASE TO
THE UNITED STATES (RECORDS OF THE OFFICE OF THE SECRETARY
OF DEFENSE).
COPYRIGHT: GTMO IN NOLA
https://gtmoinnola.wordpress.com/portfolio/cuban-perspective-on-guantanamo-bay/

As I do every year, I did a search on Google on the 25th anniversary in 2019.
I searched for the 1994 Cuban Exodus/Guantanamo Bay Cuban Detainees. I
found the above photograph during that search.

I commented to a friend, *"wouldn't it be crazy if one day I find my family in
one of these photos"*. As I was getting ready to click to the next photograph in
the search results, I decided to zoom in.

And there we were, my mother, my sister and I (see below).

MY SISTER EVELYN (CAMERA IN HAND)
NEXT TO HER HALF OF MY FACE IS VISIBLE
MY MOTHER IDALMIS

RESOURCES

National Domestic Violence Hotline

800-799-7233

https://www.thehotline.org/

Suicide and Crisis Lifeline

988

https://988lifeline.org/

Suicide Prevention for LGBTQIA+

1-866-488-7386

https://www.thetrevorproject.org/

ACKNOWLEDGEMENTS

First and foremost, thank YOU, truly, from the bottom of my heart for taking the time to read this deeply personal story. It means more to me than words can express.

To my mom: you are the most incredible mother a daughter could ever ask for. I cannot thank you enough for everything you have done for me. Without a doubt, I would not be the person I am today if it weren't for you. You endured so much in life, and you deserve every bit of happiness this world has to offer.

To my sister, Evelyn: this book would not exist without your impeccable memory. Writing this reminded me of just how much you looked out for me in the detention camps. If I've never said it before, I'm saying it now, thank you for being my protector, my confidant and my sister.

To my father: there are two things in this life I will always thank you for, one of which is the sacrifices you made to get us to this country. Regardless of everything else, none of it diminishes the fact that we are here because of you.

To my children: I hope that you will always be proud to call me your mom. I love you more than words could ever capture.

TO MY LIFELONG FRIENDS:

ACKNOWLEDGEMENTS

Samantha: I still can't believe we've been friends for twenty-five years. We may not talk every day, and we rarely see each other, but we always pick up where we left off. You are my family; you are my sister. I know you will be proud of this because I've only been saying for years that I would write it. Also, thank you for sharing dad with me. I will forever be grateful for that because he was the one that showed me what a father was truly supposed to be and for that I will always love him and call him *dad.*

Melina: nineteen years of friendship and counting. I still can't tell you enough how much I love and appreciate you.

Larissa, my very first friend: at a time when I was constantly bullied, you were the first person to show me kindness. You were my first friend, and I don't know if I ever properly thanked you, so thank you. Without you, I might have believed all American kids were cruel.

To the Bookstagram community: your support and encouragement have been nothing short of mind-blowing. I am forever grateful.

Kristen Hamilton (@kristenreadswhat): thank you for all the advice you gave me when I started my Bookstagram account and for your ongoing support. You are truly the hype woman for indie authors.

ACKNOWLEDGEMENTS

Miranda Valentine (@authormirandav): my very first author friend. Such a small world to find out we lived twenty minutes apart and I'm so glad the author universe brought us together. Thank you for all your help and guidance through the indie publishing process.

Stacy Teet (@just.me.st): my first Bookstagram friend. I still can't believe this book is out in the world. You were there from the very beginning, even reading the original college papers that inspired this memoir. Thank you for always supporting me.

Lorissa Padilla (@lorissapadilladesigns): this cover means more to me than I can ever explain. I am so grateful for the vision and talent you poured into bringing it to life.

 And finally, **Ms. Shane,** wherever you are, thank you for believing in my story and encouraging me to write it all those years ago. I truly hope someday you get to read this.

There are so many other Bookstagrammers and indie authors I could mention, but this would end up longer than most of my chapters! If we've ever chatted about books and life, shared posts, or encouraged one another along the way, thank you. I am so grateful to be part of this community.

ACKNOWLEDGEMENTS

Finally, to anyone going through a difficult time: keep pushing forward. You are stronger than you know, and you can get through it.

ABOUT THE AUTHOR

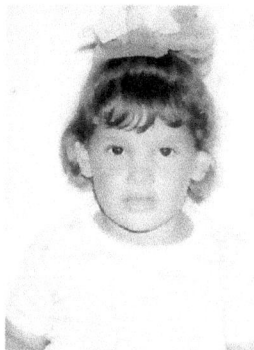

Celia is a Navy Veteran currently living in North Florida. She is a passionate storyteller, book lover, and creator who first found her voice as a bookstagrammer, sharing her love for books and for words and the way they shape our lives. She is an indie published author whose work spans genres. From her memoir, to a thoughtfully designed daily planner and journal, to the vulnerable and healing poetry collection The Gentle Rise.

Through her writing, Celia invites readers to explore life's hardest endings and most beautiful beginnings. Her work reflects her belief that words can mend, inspire, and remind us that no matter how broken we may feel, rising is always possible.

When she's not writing or connecting with fellow readers, Celia works in Corporate Operations and enjoys spending time and making memories with her daughters and her girlfriend.

She is currently working on her debut fiction novel.

CONNECT WITH THE AUTHOR

INSTAGRAM

TIKTOK

CONNECT WITH THE AUTHOR

LINKTREE

Please consider leaving a review on
Amazon and Goodreads

THANK
you

OTHER WORKS
BY THIS AUTHOR

Daily Reflections Planner and Journal

Discover the perfect companion for your day to day with this Daily Planner and Journal. The pages within offer you a space to plan your day while nurturing your creativity and reflection.

FEATURES:

- Daily Planning Pages: Structured to keep you organized with a daily quote and sections for priority tasks, other tasks, meals, and a 5am-11:30pm schedule.
- Daily Journal Pages: For inspiration and reflection with suggestion prompts to spark creativity and mindfulness.

Whether you're aiming to boost productivity, cultivate mindfulness, or simply stay organized, this Daily Planner and Journal is your essential tool for success. Embrace each day with intention and creativity!

OTHER WORKS BY THIS AUTHOR

The Gentle Rise Poetry Collection

The Gentle Rise is a journey through heartbreak, healing, and rediscovery.

Through intimate and moving poetry, interwoven with raw, reflective journal entries, Celia E. Ochoa captures the pain of endings, the courage it takes to rise again, and the quiet strength found in rebuilding a shattered heart.

For anyone who has lost, loved, and dared to hope again, this collection is a gentle reminder that even after the hardest falls, renewal and love await.